WITHDRAWN

Gramley Library
Salem College
Winston-Salem, NC 27108

WITHDRAWN

Studies in German Literature, Linguistics,
and Culture:
Literary Criticism in Perspective

Lessing's *Nathan the Wise*

Literary Criticism in Perspective

James Hardin (*South Carolina*), General Editor

Eitel Timm (*British Columbia*), German Literature

Benjamin Franklin V (*South Carolina*), American and
English Literature

Reingard M. Nischik (*Mainz*), Comparative Literature

About *Literary Criticism in Perspective*

Books in the series *Literary Criticism in Perspective*, a sub-series of *Studies in German Literature, Linguistics, and Culture* and its sister series in American and English literature, trace literary scholarship and criticism on major and neglected writers alike, or on a single major work, a group of writers, a literary school or movement. In so doing the authors — authorities on the topic in question who are also well-versed in the principles and history of literary criticism — address a readership consisting of scholars, students of literature at the graduate and undergraduate level, and the general reader. One of the primary purposes of the series is to illuminate the nature of literary criticism itself, to gauge the influence of social and historic currents on aesthetic judgments once thought objective and normative.

Jo-Jacqueline Eckardt

Lessing's *Nathan the Wise* and the Critics: *1779–1991*

CAMDEN HOUSE

Gramley Library
Salem College
Winston-Salem, NC 27108

Copyright © 1993 by
CAMDEN HOUSE, INC.

Published by Camden House, Inc.
Drawer 2025
Columbia, SC 29202 USA

Printed on acid-free paper.
Binding materials are chosen for strength and
durability.

All Rights Reserved
Printed in the United States of America
First Edition

ISBN:1-879751-43-7

Library of Congress Cataloging-in-Publication Data

Eckardt, Jo-Jacqueline, 1961-
   Lessing's Nathan the Wise and the critics, 1779-1991 / Jo
-Jacqueline Eckardt.
      p.   cm. -- (Studies in German literature, linguistics, and
culture) (Literary criticism in perspective)
   Includes bibliographical references and index.
   ISBN 1-879751-43-7 (alk. paper)
   1. Lessing, Gotthold Ephraim, 1729-1781. Nathan der Weise.
I. Title. II. Series. III. Series: Studies in German literature, linguistics,
and culture (Unnumbered)
PT2399.E25 1993
832'.6--dc20   93-4059
                                                                  CIP

Acknowledgments

I WOULD LIKE TO thank Jessica Chalmers who proofread the manuscript and offered valuable suggestions; and Volkmar and Margaret Sander who supported and encouraged my efforts.

J.-J. E.
April 1993

Contents

Introduction

NATHAN DER WEISE [NATHAN THE WISE] is the best-known play of the German writer and dramatist Gotthold Ephraim Lessing. It was written in 1779, when the author was fifty years old, two years before his death. The play takes place in Jerusalem in the era of the Crusades, toward the end of the twelfth century. Pressed for money to support his troops, the sultan Saladin turns for help to the rich merchant Nathan, known as Nathan the Wise. Following the advice of his sister Sittah, Saladin does not ask for money directly. Instead, he puts Nathan's wisdom to a test. He asks him which of the three religions — Islam, Judaism, or Christianity — is the most convincing. Nathan does not want to insult the sultan, a Moslem, nor does he want to betray his own religion, Judaism. He therefore responds to Saladin by telling him a "fairy tale," a parable about three rings that Lessing adapted from Giovanni Boccaccio's *Decamerone* (1348-1353). In ancient times, recounts Nathan, a ring was passed down the generations from father to son until the chain was broken by a father of three sons who did not want to favor one over the others. To resolve his problem he had three rings made, all indistinguishable from the original, and gave them out to his sons. When the father died, each brother had reason to believe that he possessed the original ring. A judge was called upon and gave the following advice to the brothers: each should hold onto his ring and each should keep believing in his own ring's power to bring its owner the friendship of his fellows. One day, the judge finished by saying, in a thousand years perhaps, a wiser man than he might solve their argument. Nathan succeeds in embarrassing Saladin with his parable and thereby convinces him that his question cannot be answered. As with the three rings, Saladin understands, the three religions cannot be compared.

Saladin is even more impressed with Nathan when, later in the play, Nathan identifies two long-lost family members of Saladin's and Sittah's. A young Christian Templar captured by Saladin's troops was awaiting death when Saladin, moved by the Templar's resemblance to Saladin's own brother, gave him his freedom. Through information given to him by a Lay Brother, Nathan succeeds in putting the puzzle together. The Templar really is, unbeknownst to himself, the son of Saladin's brother. Furthermore, Nathan's daughter Recha is the Templar's sister and thus Saladin's and Sittah's niece. Nathan had adopted her as a way of reconciling himself to Providence after his wife and sons were murdered by Christians. Before all the relationships are revealed, however, Nathan's safety is put in jeopardy. Daja, Recha's wet nurse, tells the Templar about Recha's origin. Not knowing the whole truth she presents the adoption in a bad light. She believes Recha to be a Christian who was robbed of her religion by Nathan's upbringing. The Templar, infatuated with Recha, carries the news of her alleged Christian origin to the Patriarch, the representative of Christianity in Jerusalem. In his fanaticism, the Patriarch demands that the Jew be found and burned. The Templar refrains from divulging Nathan's identity. In the last scene the family is united and all suspicions and prejudices seem forgotten.

As simple as the moral of the play may appear at first reading, *Nathan the Wise* has over time provoked quite contradictory reactions. This response is not surprising, however, when one considers that Lessing himself has been viewed in quite contradictory ways. He has been characterized as a devout Christian, atheist, revolutionary, conservative, national hero, a representative of the "better" Germany, poetic genius, writer lacking poetic spirit, the founder of German literature, and an isolated and unrecognized avant-gardist.

Today there exists an abundance of volumes that sample the criticism on Lessing, each documenting the wide range of interpretations to which his work has been subjected. Books concentrating particularly on *Nathan the Wise* include Klaus Bohnen's collection of critical essays (1984). Hans-Friedrich Wessels' *Lessing's "Nathan der Weise": Seine Wirkungsgeschichte bis zum Ende der Goethezeit* [Lessing's "Nathan the Wise": Its Reception until the End of the Goethe Period] (1979) goes beyond the mere compilation of texts, analyzing the individual reviews within their historical context. Unfortunately, Wessels's book is too detailed for the general reader and only covers the period up to 1830. Sigrid Suesse-Fiedler's *Lessings "Nathan der Weise" und seine Leser: Eine wirkungsästhetische Studie* [Lessing's "Nathan the Wise" and its Readers: A reception aesthetic study] (1980), on the other hand, only gives a short synopsis of past criticism. Instead, her work attempts to uncover the intended message behind the play and to show how Lessing manipulated the reader to produce a desired effect.

This book hopes to fill a gap by presenting the most pertinent interpretations of Lessing's *Nathan the Wise* chronologically, shedding light on the historical context of each critic's writing and on his or her ideological orientation. The chronological presentation of criticism traces the sometimes contradictory views of different time periods and theorists, even though it quickly becomes apparent that certain motifs and themes recur throughout the centuries like a red thread. Aspects of the play's reception such as book sales, stage performances, and its use in the classroom are, of course, important factors in the "institution" of literature. However, the primary focus is on major literary critics' interpretation of the text.

To make sense of *Nathan the Wise* today readers must go beyond the question of what Lessing wanted to say. The history of its reception sheds light not only on general trends in German literary criticism but also on the historical development of certain interpretations and expectations that have influenced every new generation of viewers and critics, including our own.

1: The Contemporary Reception

a: Lessing Criticism before 1779

WHEN *NATHAN THE WISE* appeared in 1779, Gotthold Ephraim Lessing had long been recognized as one of the leading figures of German intellectual life.[1] His reputation as a writer was as great as his reputation as a critic and literary theorist. Among the characteristics most often praised by his contemporaries are his knowledge of languages and literature, his wisdom, his critical mind, and his eloquent style of writing. In 1761 a critic in the *Bibliographie der schönen Wissenschaften und der freyen Künste* referred to him as an author so well known that the public would unhesitatingly buy any new book of his. Hans-Friedrich Wessels, a modern critic, corroborates this claim when he points out that only Klopstock may have enjoyed a similarly prepossessed interest (1979, 14). Lessing's fame soon spread to other countries, Switzerland, Austria, and France among them.

Before we turn to the reception of *Nathan the Wise*, Lessing's last dramatic work, it may be helpful to look at the reaction his earlier dramas had provoked; these reviews certainly influenced the reader's expectations in 1779. Lessing's early comedies, and especially his first tragedy, *Miss Sara Sampson* — Germany's first "bourgeois" tragedy — elevated Lessing to the level of one of the country's major writers. Some contemporaries, however, caviled at his early play *Die Juden* [The Jews] and its portrayal of a "good" Jew (Michaelis 1754).[2] *Minna von Barnhelm* appeared in 1767, first in book form and then on stage. Immediately after its publication critics hailed it as a play of national

---

[1] Lessing was famous more among his fellow intellectuals than among the general public. These intellectuals, although few in number, were the ones who shaped the social and political life of the time (cf. Raschdau 1979, 45; Berghahn 1985, 18). Habermas notes that the literary public ("Öffentlichkeit") of the eighteenth century provided a testing ground for the political debates of the nineteenth century ([17]1987, 44).

[2] Michaelis did not stand alone in his doubts about whether a positive portrayal of a Jew might be too unrealistic. Karl Lessing, Gotthold Ephraim's younger brother, is certainly not correct when he says four decades later that Michaelis's position could only provoke laughter today — that is, in 1795 (Karl Lessing 1795, II 347). This optimistic, or rather naive, statement is, in fact, not true even one hundred years later.

significance, as the long-awaited fully *German* play. This judgment was made primarily on the basis of the play's aesthetic aspects — its language and the naturalness and originality of the characters and the plot. Horst Steinmetz, the editor of a collection of critical essays on *Minna von Barnhelm*, writes that most critics welcomed the play as renewed proof of Lessing's mastership and as the first sign of the birth of a national literature (1979, 6). They saw Lessing's disregard for the dramatic unities as a liberation from the French theatrical ideal. The play's political and social implications, on the other hand, were largely ignored (cf. Barner *et al.* [5]1987, 271). The story itself did not receive much praise. While the military atmosphere and the topic of "honor" were largely welcome,[3] Tellheim himself did not win much sympathy. Likewise, Minna offended Josef Freiherr von Sonnenfels, an Austrian politician, officer, and writer, who considered her too affected (1768, 64). The minor characters, on the other hand, seem to have been received with more enthusiasm in these early reviews. The servants and subordinates in the play turned out to be the favorites of audiences and critics alike. Theatrical productions such as the Berlin staging by the Döbbelin company stressed this "popular" aspect (cf. Labus 1936?, 37ff.). The initial excitement over the play soon died down, however, as soldier plays and operettas, some of them obviously influenced by *Minna von Barnhelm*, flooded the stages. Wilfried Barner quotes a source that counts 260 plays containing similarities to *Minna von Barnhelm* before 1822 (Barner *et al.* [5]1987, 274f.). These sentimental plays contained characters similar to the popular ones in *Minna von Barnhelm*. They became the true successes of late eighteenth century drama. But whereas *Minna von Barnhelm* had excited both intellectuals and the "people," the new plays did not have such broad appeal. Once more the critics, considering themselves connoisseurs, lamented the "bad taste" of the public. They rarely got pleasure out of public theater performances. Instead, they enjoyed private readings and performances at the "Liebhabertheater," a forum created by and for the upper classes. Here *Minna von Barnhelm* as well as *Emilia Galotti* were frequently performed (cf. Barner *et al.* [5]1987, 276f). In fact, Lessing was a writer primarily for intellectuals, and *Minna von Barnhelm* — seen or read by approximately 0.5 percent of the population (cf. Raschdau 1979, 44) — was as close as he got to a "popular" success. Lessing's other great play of that period was *Emilia Galotti*, published in 1772. It never enjoyed quite the popularity that *Minna von Barnhelm* had. The immediate reaction to the publication of *Emilia Galotti* ranged from radical rejection to highest praise (Dvoretzky 1963, 111; Henning 1981, 401; Barner *et al.* [5]1987, 355-370;

---

[3] Cf. an anonymous review in the *Berlinische, privilegirte Zeitung* (April 9, 1767) that starts with the words "Hier ist alles Soldat."

Bauer 1987, 85). Eventually, however, the advocates of the play asserted themselves to the extent that *Emilia Galotti* was recognized as a masterpiece.

Wulf Rüskamp summarizes the reception of *Minna von Barnhelm* and *Emilia Galotti* in a systematic way by using critical reviews of both plays as they appeared in the literary magazines of the time. Basing his findings on Sulzer's *Allgemeine Theorie der schönen Künste* [General Theory of the Fine Arts] (1792-1799), he groups the reviews under six sometimes overlapping categories (1984, 317ff.). Depending on how they view literature, the authors focused on (1) entertainment, (2) sentimental emotions, (3) emotions following a moral goal, (4) didactic morality, (5) political aspects, or (6) aesthetics. Rüskamp does not stop at presenting the criticism schematically; he also compares it to Lessing's intentions — as he understands them. After a thorough analysis of Lessing's theoretical writing, Rüskamp concludes that Lessing's oeuvre is intended to be read for its political message. Lessing's contemporaries, however, were far more interested in entertainment, sentimentality, and morality. It is to express this idea, that Lessing's plays were never received as their author had hoped, that Rüskamp calls his book *Dramaturgie ohne Publikum* [Dramaturgy without a Public]. Jochen Schulte-Sasse, another modern critic, reaches a similar conclusion in a careful analysis of the literary structure of *Emilia Galotti* (1975). He uncovers how the play broke through the political, social, and literary expectations of its time (66). This interpretation would explain the irritation apparent in many of the contemporary reviews. It seems that most critics did not address political questions and instead restricted themselves to writing about the formal aspects of the work. Rüskamp concludes that most of the essays he examined in his book fall under the sixth category, the aesthetic one. Christine Raschdau confirms this finding: out of twenty-five texts she analyzes, only two *do not* refer to form (Raschdau 1979, 127). Rüskamp's model is more helpful in understanding eighteenth-century criticism than, for example, is that of Dvoretzky, who groups criticism according to literary schools such as Enlightenment or Storm and Stress (1963). Rüskamp's classification allows for the differences between popular criteria (entertainment or sentimentality) and the "expert" ones (neglecting content in favor of "meaning" and/or form). As we have seen, *Minna von Barnhelm* and *Emilia Galotti* found followers in both camps.

In summary, some of the basic tenets of the Lessing criticism were in place before 1779. Lessing was praised as a classical writer (Ramler 1772), as the author of masterpieces (Wieland 1772), and especially as the author of truly *German* plays.[4] Lessing was hailed as the greatest poet, a German Shake-

---

[4] Johann Joachim Eschenburg in a review dated 1767 calls *Minna von Barnhelm* "ein wahres Original, worin alles deutsch ist, nicht allein die Namen, sondern auch Handlung und Charaktere."

speare (Biester 1777). On the other hand, there were also doubts about Lessing's poetic genius. Moses Wessely (1772) is only one of the critics who complained about Lessing's work as being too cold and too rational.

b: Reviews of *Nathan the Wise*

Nathan the Wise must be understood in the context of the so-called Fragmentenstreit. In 1770 Lessing left Hamburg and his position as Dramaturg — his dream of creating a "Nationaltheater" had failed — and accepted the invitation of Duke Karl Wilhelm Ferdinand von Braunschweig to take charge of the famous and richly stocked library in Wolfenbüttel. Wolfenbüttel was a small town, even for eighteenth-century Germany, and the librarian's duties entailed a lot of routine work that, to some extent, stifled Lessing's creative impulses. It is quite obvious that he suffered from spells of depression. But Lessing's job may not have been as demeaning and boring as it is sometimes portrayed, and he was not as isolated as his geographical situation implies. He received visitors, he went on trips, and he kept up a lively correspondence with some of the more prominent personalities of eighteenth-century Germany. Also, his job gave him the opportunity to use the library for his own research. In 1773 he published the first *Beiträge zur Geschichte und Literatur* [Contributions on History and Literature] — for which the duke had granted him exemption from censorship — and invited comments and criticism. But as had been the case so many times before when Lessing had wanted to present new ideas, he provoked quarrels. The publication of the *Fragmente eines Unbekannten* (in 1774 and 1777) in the *Beiträge* was followed by the biggest dispute in which he was ever involved.

The anonymous fragments were not, as Lessing claimed, found in the Wolfenbüttel library but rather were taken from *Apologie oder Schutzschrift für die vernünftigen Verehrer Gottes* [Apologia for the Rational Worshipers of God] by Hermann Samuel Reimarus. Reimarus, a scholar of theology and ancient languages who had died in 1768, had written openly on religion from a traditional viewpoint. In the secretly written *Apologie*, however, he took a "Deist" position in favor of natural religion. The Deist philosophy which originated in England and France — John Toland and John Locke are two thinkers associated with this school — challenged religious dogmas, such as Divine Revelation, from a rational perspective. The Deists were vigorously attacked and, in eighteenth-century Germany, even persecuted. It was thus for good reason that Reimarus did not publish the *Apologie* during his lifetime. In the work he denied that the Bible was written by God, that it was to be taken literally, and lastly, that Jesus was the son of God.[5]

Even though Lessing did not publish the *Fragmente* as if they reflected his own viewpoint, he was bitterly attacked by Protestants such as Johann Daniel Schumann and Johann Heinrich Ress. Scholars have repeatedly emphasized that Lessing did not intend orthodox Protestants to be his primary opponents. They were the ones, however, who reacted. In 1778 Johann Melchior Goeze joined the orthodox camp and the dispute escalated (cf. Bollacher 1978, 42-202; Barner *et al.* [5]1987, 291-309). Lessing wrote several articles, known as the *Anti-Goeze*, defending his own position. At this point, Duke Karl's administration revoked Lessing's exemption from censorship. Lessing was told to refrain from publishing any further fragments or comments in the matter. When Lessing's articles then began to appear in other cities, the duke reissued his decree to include all of Germany. It was under these conditions that Lessing decided to finish *Nathan the Wise*, a play he had begun many years earlier.

When Lessing announced his decision to publish a play and solicit subscriptions in August 1778, the response was overwhelming. Wessels coins the term "Wirkung ohne Werk" for this phenomenon: an enormous reaction to a work that has not yet been published (Wessels 1979, 14). The public had followed the "Fragmentenstreit" closely. Many articles appeared in defense of the orthodox or of Lessing's position; a third group refrained from agreeing with either side, while acknowledging Lessing's superior style. Everyone, however, awaited the new play, curious to see what the controversial Lessing would come up with next. Some anticipated a satirical play or a theological comedy, others counted on a serious drama (cf. Wessels 1979, 21-23; cf. also a letter by Friedrich Wilhelm Gotter of September 24, 1778).

When *Nathan the Wise* finally appeared at the Leipzig Easter Fair in 1779, it was an immediate success — Wessels calculates that approximately 3,000 copies were sold, more than of any comparable work at that time (1979, 28f.). In a letter to Hamann in May 1779, Herder testifies that *Nathan the Wise* was indeed "devoured." New editions and pirated editions followed. Because the play was so widely discussed, reviewers frequently omitted a synopsis of it, assuming that the readers were already acquainted with its plot (*Staats- und Gelehrte Zeitung* 1779; *Kaiserlich privilegirte Hamburgische Neue Zeitung* 1779; *Gothaische gelehrte Zeitungen* 1779; *Kielisches Litteratur-Journal* 1780). *Nathan the Wise*'s success, however, was with the intellectuals more than with the general public, just as had been the case with *Emilia Galotti*.

---

[5] For an English translation of the *Fragmente*, see Talbert 1970, 61-269. The German text can also be found in Specht 1986, 202-247. For an analysis of the relation between Reimarus and *Nathan the Wise*, see Timm 1989.

Therefore, Dieter Arendt's dictum that *Nathan the Wise* was "ein literarisches Ereignis [a literary event]," is a fitting one: *Nathan the Wise* was a great event, though limited to the literary world (D. Arendt [4]1990, 59).

Most reviews appeared in journals published in northern and eastern Germany (in Hamburg, Kiel, Berlin, Gotha, and Nürnberg). Many of these reviews praised the drama as a masterpiece,[6] as a work worthy of Lessing (*Staats- und Gelehrte Zeitung* 1779; *Neueste Critische Nachrichten* 1779; *Kaiserlich privilegirte Hamburgische Neue Zeitung* 1779). Aesthetic aspects such as the dialogue (cf. *Kielisches Litteratur-Journal* 1780), the iambic verse (*Der teutsche Merkur* 1780), and the characters were praised. Some reviewers noted that each character spoke his or her "own language" (*Nürnbergische gelehrte Zeitung* 1779; *Neue Zeitungen von gelehrten Sachen* 1779). Nathan especially impressed critics as noble and wise: "Einen weiseren Mann gabs wol mal nie [there never was a wiser man]" (*Neuer Gelehrter Mercurius* 1779). Johann Georg Jacobi noticed the "newness" of the play (1779). If there was any negative aesthetic criticism, it was to point out a few "cold" (*Nürnbergische gelehrte Zeitung*, 1779) or "bitter" passages (*Neueste Critische Nachrichten*, 1779). Despite the positive reception, there was a general concern that the play would probably not be performed because of its length and unconventionality.

Separate from aesthetic and formal considerations were questions regarding the drama's content. Herein lay the true sensation. After all, the publication of *Nathan the Wise* came after a heated theological debate between Lessing and Goeze. Few critics dared to take a firm stand on either side. Some admitted that they did not consider themselves fit to decide, and others simply referred the reader to the play, which, they said, spoke for itself (*Nürnbergische gelehrte Zeitung* 1779; *Kielisches Litteratur-Journal* 1780). Hans-Friedrich Wessels has analyzed the pertinent documents[7] and finds only five that explicitly took a stand in the theological dispute. It is probable that the writers who were inclined to side with Lessing disguised their approval for fear of repercussions (1979, 45f.; 69-72). It is interesting in this respect to look at the magazines that did *not* review *Nathan the Wise*: Boie's important *Deutsches Museum*, for example. This omission is all the more surprising since Boie

---

[6] The term "Meisterstück" can be found in several reviews: *Königl. privilegirte Staats- und gelehrte Zeitung* (1779); *Allgemeine deutsche Bibliothek* (1782, 111). Goethe is also said to have called it that, as Friedrich Heinrich Jacobi writes in a letter to Heinse in 1780.

[7] Two reviews of Wessels's count are not included in Braun (1884): the *Königsbergische gelehrte und politische Zeitung* (May 18, 1780), and *Frankfurter gelehrte Anzeigen* (May 28, 1779).

privately wrote positively about the play. Only in letters and diaries did writers approve of *Nathan the Wise* (cf. Wessels 1979, 73-77). Even friends and supporters of Lessing refrained from speaking publicly on his behalf (among them Johann Georg Hamann, Else Reimarus, Joachim Heinrich Campe, and Johann Wilhelm Ludwig Gleim).

The *Beytrag zum Reichs-Post-Reuter* (1780) wrongly complained about the lack of negative reaction to *Nathan the Wise*. Orthodox Protestants made no secret of their outrage: they considered Raimarus's *Fragments* as well as Lessing's *Nathan the Wise* blasphemous and dangerous. Despite Lessing's assurances that the Patriarch was not to be identified with Goeze, the similarities were obvious to his contemporaries. The anonymous reviewer of the *Beytrag* called *Nathan the Wise* a "Satire gegen die christliche Religion [satire against the Christian religion]." Even people who were less orthodox in their beliefs found Lessing's position questionable at best and avoided associating with him. To many, the choice of a Jewish protagonist alone was an insult to Christianity.

One of the more fervid critics of Lessing was Balthasar Ludewig Tralles. He published his two-volume work *Zufällige alt-deutsche und christliche Betrachtungen über Hrn. Gotthold Ephraim Lessings Gedicht Nathan der Weise* [Incidental old-German and Christian Comments on Mr. Lessing's Poem *Nathan the Wise*] only a few months after Lessing's play appeared in 1779. In the introduction dated August 10, 1779, Tralles expresses his indignation over what he saw as Lessing's undisguised ridicule of religion (I, 4). He begins his invective with a pedantic analysis of the play's "un-German" language. How could a foreigner possibly learn the German language if writers kept adding new words at their fancy? asks Tralles (10). He works through the play page by page, suggesting corrections and changes, and explaining passages. Tralles then tackles the theological implications of the play, again going through the text page by page. The contemporaries who attacked Tralles partly based their criticism on his method: how he takes every word literally, how he does not acknowledge that each character holds a different position but instead expects every position to represent Lessing's own point of view. Nathan asks rhetorically whether man is not more than Christian or Jew; Tralles ponders this question and then answers in the negative (43). The idea that humans are made equal or that to be human is of the highest value is totally foreign to Tralles, whom the Enlightenment seems to have bypassed. According to Tralles, to be human is simply not enough. One must be a Christian first. Reason — and Tralles uses this Enlightenment term for his own purposes — proves that Christianity is the one true religion, and that the Bible contains no tales and fables (54f.) He is incensed that Lessing could have rejected Christianity while favoring Jews and Turks (93). Underlying Tralles's argument is an idea that was also expressed by Goeze: that religion is needed to uphold law and order

(69); to mock religion is to mock the state. Like Goeze before him, Tralles blames Lessing for courting the downfall of morality by making fun of the Christian faith. It goes without saying that Tralles rejects the "Ringparabel." His reasoning is that since Christianity is the true religion, the father, were he to symbolize God, should have marked the original ring in such a way as to separate it from the copies (50). Because Lessing failed to have him do so, the parable does not convince Tralles. He dismisses Nathan's telling of the parable as a cowardly act of intrigue (46). Tralles may well be the only critic who has ever defended Daja, the Christian wet nurse of Recha: he claims that she is just as good a person as Nathan (81-83). It is hard to decide in retrospect whether Tralles' position could be called anti-Semitic in the racist sense that has developed since the nineteenth century. Tralles sees the Jew as a representative of a different religion, not race, and generously grants that there are some good people among them. Tellingly, however, the one Jew Tralles is favorably impressed by is one who has begun the assimilation process: he has accepted the Christian Lord's prayer as his own (97). Tralles's "well-meant" compliment to the Jews reveals his underlying lack of regard for them.

Only a few contemporary critics dared to openly defend Lessing against such attacks. Among them is the author of "Briefe an Madame B," which appeared in the *Litteratur- und Theater Zeitung* in 1780-1781. Franklin Kopitzsch believes the author of the letters to be Christian Gottfried Schütz - not Friedrich Wilhelm von Schütz, as is widely believed (1975, 86). People, Schütz says in his letters, should be allowed to believe in the religion they are born into since salvation cannot depend on dogma but on pleasing God — and pleasing God can be done in any religion (Schütz 1780-1781, 334f.). At the same time, Schütz defends the play against unfair criticism. One should not, he writes, take every word of Nathan's to be an expression of Lessing's own opinion.

Another manner of defending Nathan was by claiming that his Jewishness was of no importance. Whether this well-intended defense was not just another expression of early forms of anti-Semitism is another question. Nathan is not particularly "Jewish" and may as well be a Christian, says the reviewer for the *Nürnbergische gelehrte Zeitung* (1779). The *Allgemeine deutsche Bibliothek* (1782?) attempts to deemphasize Lessing's attack on orthodox theology. Nathan, the reviewer argues, merely fought the "Schwärmerey [fanaticism]" in both his daughter and the Patriarch (110), but he did not want to criticize Christianity. The most outspoken defense of Lessing came from the *Auserlesene Bibliothek der neuesten deutschen Litteratur* (1780). The anonymous reviewer dares to name Lessing's attackers calling them the "schwachköpfigten Hyperorthodoxen [dumb hyper-orthodox]." He denounces Lessing's critics as naughts but praises *Nathan the Wise* as a monument of progress.

c: Theatrical Responses

As Lessing himself had predicted in a letter to his brother Karl on April 18, 1779 (Lessing 1970-1979, II 723), the theaters were reluctant to perform *Nathan the Wise*. Censorship played a role, but so did doubts about whether the play would be a success. It seemed too long and too demanding, not just for the viewers but for the actors and stage designers as well. During Lessing's lifetime, there were only a couple of private readings and performances. *Nathan the Wise* finally premiered on April 14, 1783, two years after Lessing's death, in Berlin. But the Döbbelin company did not repeat the huge success of *Minna von Barnhelm* several years earlier and *Nathan the Wise* was performed only three times. As during Lessing's lifetime, productions until the turn of the century consisted mainly of readings or private stagings by "Liebhabergesell-schaften" (cf. Ursula Schulz 1977, 192; Wessels 1979, 248f.).

The general public, then, did not get a chance to see *Nathan the Wise*, but it did have the opportunity of seeing the many plays and parodies written in reaction to Lessing's drama.[8] The most important was Johann Georg Pfranger's *Der Mönch vom Libanon* [The Monk from Lebanon] (1782). Pfranger, a priest, did not write a parody but instead attempted a benevolent "correction" of what he deemed the expression of a "stray" mind. *Der Mönch vom Libanon* picks up the story where Lessing left off. Believing himself dying, Saladin is tormented by a guilty conscience and, ever since Nathan told him the story of the rings, by doubts about his faith. Nathan still plays an important role, though in this play he appears more cunning than "wise." As main character and hero, he is replaced by a mysterious monk who only reveals his true identity in the end. He is Assad, Saladin's brother and thus the father of Recha and the Templar; he is assumed to be dead in *Nathan the Wise* but is, obviously, still alive in Pfranger's play. Assad has converted to Christianity and become a monk. As the play's protagonist, he embodies all the virtues Pfranger wished to bestow on a good Christian. Two entirely new characters are also introduced. They are evil Moslems who carry out a doomed intrigue against Saladin. Central to the play, finally, is a parable about agriculture, replacing Lessing's ring story. Assad tells it before revealing his identity. Pfranger intends his parable to settle the question of true religion

---

[8] Wessels declares *Nathan the Wise* comparable only to Goethe's *Werther* as far as literary impact is concerned (1979, 281). This claim seems a little out of proportion: the 13 imitations and parodies Wessels refers to do not even come close to the 260 plays (up to 1822) that followed in the succession of *Minna von Barnhelm* (cf. Barner *et al.* [5]1987, 274f.).

once and for all in favor of Christianity. *Der Mönch vom Libanon*, at first published anonymously, was relatively successful and was reissued several times into the nineteenth century (Wessels 1979, 282).

As mentioned above, many of the plays written in the wake of *Nathan the Wise* were satirical parodies. Some telling titles are *Der travestirte Nathan der Weise* [The Travestied Nathan the Wise] by Julian von Voß (1804), and *Nathan der Dumme* [Nathan the Dumb] (anonymous, no date; cf. Lea 1991, 173-175). These plays used sentiments against Jews as a major component of their satire. There were, however, also plays whose authors supported Jewish emancipation. Charlene A. Lea draws attention to the "appearance of the positively portrayed Jewish stereotype in at least fifty plays between 1749 and 1805" (1991, 166). The "noble Jew" appeared in several plays, usually as a minor character. Lessing, then, was not the first to present Jewish characters in his plays; he *was* the first author, however, to avoid stereotyping them, either positively or negatively. In a recent article on the "noble Jew" in literature, Jürgen Stenzel rightly reminds his readers that creating an idealized Jewish character is just the flip side of anti-Semitism, since idealization is also based on prejudice and generalization (1986, 114).

The effects of prejudice and oppression on the Jewish community were acknowledged and discussed only reluctantly at that time, and so Christian Wilhelm Dohm's treatise *Über die bürgerliche Verbesserung der Juden* [About the Improvement of the Social Situation for the Jews] (1781) was a real groundbreaker in this respect (cf. Altmann 1973, 449-461; Wessels 1979, 306-317; Detering 1986; Rose 1990, 70-79). Dohm, a Christian, blamed the prejudice and oppression under which Jews were living for their disadvantaged status as well as for some negative characteristics he attributed to them. His book was published only two years after *Nathan the Wise*. Those two years made a difference. While *Über die bürgerliche Verbesserung der Juden* initiated a wide discussion of Jewish emancipation, the contemporary criticism of *Nathan the Wise* hardly touches on this topic. It could be argued, however, that the orthodox criticism was implicitly anti-Semitic since typically it complained that Nathan, a Jew, was portrayed in too positive a light at the expense of the Christian characters. Voices from the Jewish side, were not as audible at that time, since it might have been risky for a Jew to publicly rejoice in Lessing's play. A rumor that spread in 1779 can be understood as a warning: some journals repeated the unfounded allegation that Lessing had been paid 1,000 ducats by Amsterdam Jews in return for his favorable depiction of a Jew (cf. *Litteratur- und Theater-Zeitung* 1780). Only later, when Jews had progressed farther in their emancipation, did they claim Nathan as a symbol for their cause.

Thus it was left to non-Jewish authors to write plays in Lessing's succession. None of these plays equalled Lessing's in quality or moral ambition. The parallels and allusions to *Nathan the Wise* were often as obvious as in *Wer war wohl mehr Jude* [Who was more of a Jew?] by Karl Lotich (1783), where the good and honest Jewish protagonist Wolf is actually reading *Nathan the Wise* (cf. Stümcke 1904, xxix-xxxi; Wessels 1979, 354-360). When his daughter is pursued by a Christian, he reveals that she is really an adopted child of Christian background. Variations on this motif — a Christian girl adopted by a Jewish father — are found in a series of other dramas of the time (for example, Reinicke 1784, Sternberg 1787; cf. Stümcke 1904, xxxi-xli; Wessels 1979, 364-375). By 1805 the "noble Jew" had disappeared again from the German stage (Lea 1991, 176).

All of the plays discussed thus far take as their point of departure the plot of *Nathan the Wise*. There is another tradition, however, that was inspired by the formal elements of Lessing's drama. Lessing called *Nathan the Wise* a "dramatisches Gedicht [dramatic poem]," thereby transgressing all known genres. At the time, the debate about what that term meant was intense (cf. Wessels 1979, 51-55, 96-108, 117-124). To this day, critics are puzzled by Lessing's definition. Questions have been asked about the play's poetic value, its didactic elements, and the innovative effect it had on the dramatists after Lessing. In retrospect, *Nathan the Wise* can be seen as a forerunner of classical "Ideendramen [idea dramas]" such as Goethe's *Iphigenie*, in particular.

d: After Lessing's Death

After Gotthold Ephraim Lessing's death on February 15, 1781, criticism of individual works receded into the background. The order of the day was necrologies and appraisals of his total oeuvre. There were evaluations of Lessing's significance and of his role in intellectual history. Coins and monuments were commissioned, memorial services staged.[9] Ten years after Lessing's death his grave still lacked a tombstone, and attempts to collect for a monument in Wolfenbüttel remained fruitless until 1796 (cf. Meister 1789, 371; Großmann 1791; Danzel 1881, 624-634). If there was a general consensus, it was that Lessing deserved praise for his versatility and respect for his role in intellectual history. He was heralded as the pioneer and originator of German literature. The danger associated with this position, Klaus Bohnen convincingly argues, is that Lessing's work is not respected for its own worth

---

[9] In 1781 the *Königlich privilegirte Berlinische Zeitung* advertised a silver coin with Lessing's name, year of birth and death, an inscription, and the title of his play *Nathan the Wise*.

Gransley Library
Salem College
Winston-Salem, NC 27108

but is reduced to a mere "forerunner" of things to come, namely of Classicism (Bohnen 1982, 177f.).

One of the more important necrologies written after Lessing's death was Herder's contribution to Wieland's *Der teutsche Merkur* (1781). It was also one of the first character sketches to employ so many of the clichés that shaped Lessing's image for centuries to come: Lessing, the great German author comparable only to Luther,[10] the manly knight,[11] the loyal friend,[12] the searcher for truth.[13] Interested in philosophy and literary theory himself, Herder writes more about Lessing's theoretical than his dramatic works. *Nathan the Wise* is discussed only indirectly, in relation to the theological debate. Herder, a Christian and theologian,[14] defends Lessing's right to scrutinize and contest what was generally taken as "truth." Herder interprets Lessing's quest for truth, however, by associating it with a cold, "dispassionate passion."[15] As respectfully as this comment is phrased, there are clearly some negative implications. As a result, the idea of Lessing's lack of warmth has become axiomatic within criticism.

Late in life, Herder turned to Lessing and *Nathan the Wise* once more. In his *Adrastea* (1801) he elaborated Lessing's ideas about humanity, fate, and general tolerance. The parable of the three rings struck him as a symbolic tale, "ein Mährchen... der Menschen-, Religion- und Völkerhuldigung [a fairy tale venerating people, religions, and nations]" (119). Herder thus steered away

---

[10] "... wer schreibt ursprünglich deutscher als *Luther* oder *Lessing*?" (124).

[11] "Der blanke männliche Harnisch kleidet Lessing mehr als das Gängelband der Reime; seine Fabeln sind nicht bloß für Kinder, sondern auch Männern, und Männern insonderheit, lesbar" (125).

[12] "Lessing, der an jedem Ort jeden Würdigen gern ins Licht zog, wenn er dienen konnte, der gern diente - der männliche, tätig freundschaftliche, neidlose *Lessing* wird nicht so gar oft und viel seines gleichen haben" (130).

[13] "Und wo bist du nun, edler Wahrheitssucher, Wahrheitskenner, Wahrheitsverfechter - was siehst, was erblickst du jetzt?" (133).

[14] "Ich bin auch ein Theolog, und die Sache der Religion liegt mir so sehr am Herzen als irgendjemandem; manche Stellen und Stiche der Fragmentisten haben mir wehgetan...." (131).

[15] "Auch bei dem Irrtum ist Eifer für die Wahrheit schätzbar, − die Leidenschaft, die daher entsteht, daß man keiner Leidenschaft, keinem Truge unterworfen sein will, ist hochachtungswürdig. Nicht jeder gelangt zu dieser *warmen* Kälte, zu dieser leidenschaftlosen Leidenschaft für Wahrheit und für alles was zu ihr führet" (133).

from the theological debate over the drama. His conception of literature, one must remember, was a classical one. He was interested in ideal representations that "humanize" the reader and make him or her a better person. Herder thought that *Nathan the Wise* had a "humanizing" effect through its symbolic meaning. Because he understood *Nathan the Wise* as a symbolic play, Herder rejected the idea that it was a didactic one;[16] he preferred the term "dramatische Schicksalsfabel [dramatic fable of fate]" (118).

Several encyclopedias and biographical works of the 1780s mention Lessing. Karl August Küttner's *Charaktere teutscher Dichter und Prosaisten* [German Poets and Prose Writers] (1781) focuses mainly on Lessing's comedies. Leonhard Meister, similarly, has little to say about *Nathan the Wise* in *Charakteristik deutscher Dichter* [Characteristics of German Poets] (1789, on *Nathan the Wise* cf. esp. 367). One author who praises *Nathan the Wise* above Lessing's other dramas is Johann Jakob Hottinger (1789). In his comparison of Lessing with the ancient tragic writers, however, Lessing does not fare as well as Roman and Greek authors. Hottinger prefers the classical writers and questions Lessing's poetic genius.[17] According to his view, only *Nathan the Wise* possesses the genuine warmth that can touch the heart.

It is obvious from these documents that Moses Mendelssohn did not express the general opinion of his time when, in a condolence letter to Lessing's brother Karl, he declared *Nathan the Wise* the apex of perfection and far ahead of its time (Mendelssohn 1781, 122-123). Mendelssohn, who so often has been identified as the prototype for Nathan, was also a source of support and advice for Lessing while Lessing was working on the play. Mendelssohn read the manuscript and returned the pages to his friend not only with comments and corrections but also with enthusiastic encouragement (cf. Karl Lessing's letter to his brother on May 1, 1779, where he describes Mendelssohn's enthusiasm for *Nathan the Wise*. Mendelssohn, Karl informs his brother, called it the "best play Lessing ever wrote"). Upon hearing the news of Lessing's death, Mendelssohn was deeply shocked. He immediately resolved to write a character study that would "do justice" to his friend.[18] But the project was delayed when Mendelssohn could not get some of the

---

[16] Johann Jakob Engel calls the play in 1783 a "Lehrgedicht" (Engel 1806, 139).

[17] "Ich halte ihn, so wie er ist, für unsern ersten Tragiker, und wenn ein Dichtergenie ohne Wärme sein kann, auch für eines der ersten Dichtergenien. Er erregt meine Teilnehmung, reißt mich hin, entzückt mich, aber er wärmt mich nicht" (155).

[18] Cf. Mendelssohn's letter of May 8, 1781, to August Adolph Friedrich Hennings, translated in Altmann 1973, 587f.

letters and papers he wanted to draw on and was finally abandoned. Only a short sketch remained, appearing after Mendelssohn's death in Karl Lessing's biography of his brother (Mendelssohn 1795). In this text Mendelssohn praises Lessing's wit and his realism, although at the same time he admits that a certain lack of passion accounted for some artificiality in Lessing's writing.

One question that occupied Mendelssohn was whether or not Lessing had embraced Spinoza's idea of pantheism. Friedrich Heinrich Jacobi asserted in a letter to Mendelssohn (November 4, 1783) that Lessing had done so, basing his claim on a conversation with Lessing shortly before his death. Mendelssohn denied this notion fervently and attempted to rescue Lessing as a follower of "natural religion." Mendelssohn's *Morgenstunden, oder Vorlesungen über das Dasein Gottes* [Morning Hours; or, Lectures on the Being of God] (1785) is to be understood as a reaction to the dispute. "Though originally announced as a refutation of Spinozism, the real concern of the work was the portrayal of Lessing in a manner calculated to neutralize, if not to nullify, the effect of any future disclosures by Jacobi" (Altmann 1973, 686). Mendelssohn does not go so far as to deny any toying with Spinozist ideas on Lessing's part. He claims that Lessing could at most be called a "purified Spinozist," one who believes God and Nature to be one and to exist independently at the same time. In the fifteenth lecture of *Morgenstunden* Mendelssohn presents a fictitious dialogue between himself and an anonymous "D" to further elaborate on Lessing's theological beliefs. It is in this dialogue that Mendelssohn coins the word *Anti-Candide* to characterize *Nathan the Wise* (Mendelssohn 1785, 143). What he means is that Lessing praises divine Providence in his play, whereas Voltaire's *Candide* is a satire that is critical of the concept of Providence. To accuse Lessing of reviling Christianity is therefore, in Mendelssohn's eyes, a gross misinterpretation: "Im Grunde gereicht sein 'Nathan', wie wir uns gestehen müssen, der Christenheit zur wahren Ehre [We have to admit that, actually, Nathan does real credit to Christianity]" (Mendelssohn 1785, 144). Lessing's other close friend from his Berlin years, Christoph Friedrich Nicolai, expresses a similar thought when he says that Lessing's initial inclination to start publishing Reimarus's *Fragments* was to do a service to the Protestant orthodoxy (cf. Daunicht 1971, 379).

Yet one other person with whom Lessing was closely connected, his younger brother Karl, deemed it necessary to protest against possible orthodox accusations. In his *Gotthold Ephraim Lessings Leben* [Gotthold Ephraim Lessing's Life], he implores his Christian readers to believe that his older brother really was a true Christian and a true Lutheran:

> "Barmherzigkeit, liebe Christen, liebe Lutheraner! er war wirklich ein
> ehrlicher Christ, ein ehrlicher Lutheraner, in allem möglichen Sinne, in
> dem man diese Benennungen nehmen kann [Have mercy, dear

Christians, dear Lutherans! He really was an honest Christian, an honest Lutheran in the best possible sense of these words]" (I 441).

Karl also interprets *Nathan the Wise* in this vein. He understands it as a play directed against the delusion that one religion is better than the other, but not as a denunciation of Christianity. Even orthodox Christians, Karl entreats his readers, have conceded that their congregation might benefit from some reforms, and this idea is all Gotthold Ephraim wanted to suggest (II 393f.). This apologetic tone is characteristic of Karl's lengthy biography, which appeared in three volumes between 1793 and 1795, ten years after Gotthold Ephraim's death.

Politically, the book falls short of ideal. It reveals a conciliatory attitude toward the authorities who had banned *Nathan the Wise*. Karl sympathetically defends the Braunschweig court and its decision to censor his brother's writing (cf. I 304, 393, 411f.). This position is only weakly justified by the argument that the *Fragments* were in the end read by more people *because* it was banned (I 399f.). Discussing the above mentioned Mendelssohn-Jacobi dispute about whether Lessing was a Spinozist or not, Karl's laborious conclusion is that one can be a pantheist and a theist all at the same time (II 40f., 46). Finally, Karl, who himself tried his hand at play writing rather unsuccessfully, sides with the critics who question Gotthold Ephraim's poetic talent, especially his supposed lack of lyricism (II 14, 295, 304). Lessing was primarily a dramatic and a didactic poet, the brother writes (II, 395). The best thing that may be said about Karl Lessing's work — the first major biography of Gotthold Ephraim Lessing — is that it preserves a wealth of information, anecdotes, and quotations, especially in Volume I, that might have otherwise been lost.

2: Friedrich Schlegel and Friedrich Schiller

a: Schlegel

FRIEDRICH SCHLEGEL'S STUDIES of Lessing's work were the most influential for the nineteenth century. His 1797 *Lyceum* essay 1797 "Über Lessing [On Lessing]," in particular, is considered a turning point in Lessing criticism, although it was neither the first nor the last time that Schlegel took on this subject. It seems only natural that he would have been intrigued by an author who had worked toward a goal similar to his own. Thirty years before Schlegel called for a "progressive Universalpoesie" that would meld poetry, criticism, and rhetoric into a single textual mode, Lessing had already made the first steps toward combining literature, philosophy, and criticism. Schlegel was not, however, favorably disposed toward Lessing's project at the outset. In 1792 he writes of Lessing's coldness and correctness. It was not until 1796 that Schlegel "became converted" to Lessing (cf. Krüger 1913, esp. 36-39; Wessels 1979, 151f.).

The essay "Über Lessing" attests to Schlegel's nascent recognition of the strengths of Lessing's versatility. Schlegel claims that interdisciplinary work aims at universal understanding and progressivity, the two "romantic" virtues of art. He further notes that underlying Lessing's work as well as his own is a polemical argument. Because Schlegel presents Lessing's critical approach as representative of romantic criticism and philosophy, critics have often called "Über Lessing" characteristic of Schlegel's own romantic style more than of Lessing's (Peter 1978, 36).

Schlegel begins his essay by dismissing all other critical perspectives on Lessing's work. According to his belief, the public was holding onto a petrified image of Lessing, a "heilige Überlieferung" (170). What Schlegel objected to is what is now called *canonization*. No German scholar before Schlegel delineated so clearly the importance that the critical reception of a work has on how the work itself is generally perceived.[1] The "mediocre and fashionable" Lessing commentators, Schlegel writes, try to pull Lessing down to their level without even having read his most important works. They place the poet above the critic, Schlegel continues. They marvel at his extensive

---

[1] Cf. Seeba 1973, 151; Higonnet 1979, 95; Wessels 1979, 159. Hans Dierkes, on the other hand, denies that Schlegel functions as forerunner to modern reception theory (1980, 167-172).

knowledge and versatility, but they do not recognize his wit, his ethical stand, nor the admirable aspects of his character. Schlegel asserts that Lessing himself, were he alive, would be astounded and taken aback (171).

It has been argued that Schlegel's accusations are not quite justified. As we saw in the previous chapter, Lessing's contemporaries admired his criticism as well as his good character and moral steadfastness. Schlegel was by no means the first to consider Lessing manly, independent, firm, and dignified. The list of writers who questioned Lessing's poetic genius is also considerable, and many date from long before Schlegel published his opinion. What is more, Schlegel could not have been ignorant of this fact. Johanna Krüger (1913, 56-58) proves that Schlegel relied heavily on observations made by Johann Jakob Hottinger (1789). On the other hand, Schlegel has a point when he says that no one has yet examined how all the aspects of Lessing's life and work were intertwined: "welcher *gemeinsame Geist* alles beseelt, was er denn eigentlich *im ganzen* war, sein wollte und werden mußte [Which common spirit inspires everything; what he as a whole really was, wanted to be, and had to become]" (175). Indeed, Schlegel's was the first attempt at such a complete picture of Lessing. In making this attempt he used such memorable phrases as "Er selbst war mehr wert, als alle seine Talente [He himself was more valuable than all of his talents]" (178). This famous statement about Lessing has too often been quoted out of context and taken to mean that Lessing's achievements as a writer do not equal his moral stature. This is not quite what Schlegel meant. Schlegel saw Lessing — his character *and* his talents — as a whole and postulates that it is the combination of all his character traits, talents, and tendencies (*Tendenz* is a favorite word of Schlegel's) that make the man. This combination was, Schlegel writes, how Lessing anticipated progressive art or "Universalpoesie," as he also called his vision of a romantic art form combining poetry, philosophy, and criticism. If one looks at only a single aspect of Lessing or his work, Schlegel warns, his true essence and greatness is lost.

When he rates individual works, however, Schlegel becomes discriminating. He devises a hierarchy that pushes the poetic works and some of the dramas down toward the bottom. Lessing's true poetry, Schlegel writes, is evidenced more in his critical and polemical works. Among them, Schlegel ranks the *Anti-Goeze* highest. In this series of essays he finds genius, moral sublimity, and poetic spirit. *Emilia Galotti*, on the other hand, Lessing's "eigentliche Hauptwerk [real masterpiece]" (181), is a masterpiece of reason — and by *reason* Schlegel means to criticize the play. He writes that it was produced with sweat and pain and that it was a great example "der dramatischen Algebra [of dramatic algebra]" (182). The claim that Lessing lacked poetic warmth and spirit in his dramatic writing is backed up — as always when critics question Lessing's "genius" — by Lessing's famous self-description in the *Dramaturgie*:[2]

> Ich bin weder Schauspieler noch Dichter.
> Man erweiset mir zwar manchmal die Ehre, mich für den letztern zu erkennen. Aber nur, weil man mich verkennt. Aus einigen dramatischen Versuchen, die ich gewagt habe, sollte man nicht so freygebig folgern. Nicht jeder, der den Pinsel in die Hand nimmt, und Farben verquistet, ist ein Mahler. Die ältesten von jenen Versuchen sind in den Jahren hingeschrieben, in welchen man Lust und Leichtigkeit so gern für Genie hält. Was in den neuern erträgliches ist, davon bin ich mir sehr bewußt, daß ich es einzig und allein der Critik zu verdanken habe. Ich fühle die lebendige Quelle nicht in mir, die durch eigene Kraft sich emporarbeitet, durch eigene Kraft in so reichen, so frischen, so reinen Strahlen aufschießt: ich muß alles durch Druckwerk und Röhren aus mir herauf pressen. (Lessing 1970-1979, IV 694)
> [I am neither actor nor poet. To be sure, people sometimes do me the honor to judge me the latter. But only because they misjudge me. They should not draw such generous conclusions from a few dramatic efforts that I once ventured. Not everyone who takes brush in hand and squanders colors is a painter. The earliest of those efforts were dashed off during those years when one is so glad to consider desire and facility synonymous with genius. Whatever is acceptable in my later efforts is due solely to criticism, as I am well aware. I do not feel within me the vital spring that mounts of its own power, and of its own power shoots upward in such rich, fresh, pure streams: I must force everything up within me by pumps and pipelines. (Brown 1971, 110)]

Nathan the Wise is the one drama that Schlegel valued as highly as Lessing's critical texts. Although less polished and less "perfect" in form and convention than *Emilia Galotti*, the "peak of poetic art" (181), *Nathan the Wise* is the "peak of poetic genius" to Schlegel (182) because it combines poetry and philosophy in a novel way. This mixture is as unique to the play as to Lessing himself, and for this reason the play "represents" Lessing. Schlegel explains: "Wer den 'Nathan' recht versteht, kennt Lessing [Whoever understands 'Nathan' correctly knows Lessing]" (183). Schlegel calls the play

---

[2] Ingrid Strohschneider-Kohrs warns her readers not to take Lessing's self-description too seriously, as he probably meant it to fight off contemporary notions of what a poet should be (1981, 15).

the "Anti-Goeze number twelve"[3] and thus refers to the history of the play. In a letter to his brother Karl on August 11, 1778, Lessing expressed his intention of provoking a stronger reaction with his new play than with the fragments he had written previously against Goeze (Lessing 1970-1979, II 718f.). Schlegel understands *Nathan the Wise* as a continuation of the dispute between Lessing and Goeze. Accordingly, he emphasizes the polemical element in the play. The "Polemik gegen alle illiberale Theologie [the polemic against illiberal theology]" is one of the two "main elements" that Schlegel discerns in *Nathan the Wise* (186f.). At the same time, *Nathan the Wise* is also a poetic work to Schlegel (186). Poetry and morality are closely connected in *Nathan the Wise*, Schlegel argues (186). Schlegel does not draw upon the play's formal characteristics as evidence of its poetic value. On the contrary, he says that the dramatic form is only a vehicle for the polemic (185). The verses are sometimes even ridiculous, Schlegel finds, and yet he proclaims that *Nathan the Wise* is a "gigantic" work of poetry, "die beste *Apologie* der gesamten *Lessingschen Poesie* [the best defense of Lessing's poetry as a whole]" (1797, 188). The poetry in *Nathan the Wise* stems from its cynicism: "'Nathan der Weise' ist nicht bloß die Fortsetzung des 'Anti-Goeze', Numero zwölf: er ist auch und ist ebensosehr ein dramatisiertes Elementarbuch des höheren Zynismus [*Nathan the Wise* is not only a continuation of the *Anti-Goeze* Number twelve, it is also a dramatized elementary book of higher cynicism]" (1797, 187). Cynicism, which is closely related to irony and wit, is among the true elements of poetry in Schlegel's eyes.

Postulating *Nathan the Wise*'s basic intention as polemical was as far as Schlegel took his interpretation. He did not examine what Lessing wanted to argue for or against. On the contrary, he believes that any explanation of the "message" would be wrong and would limit this work unfairly "auf eine einzige allzubestimmte und am Ende ziemlich triviale Tendenz [to a single, too narrowly determined, ultimately rather trivial tendency]" (186). Instead, *Nathan the Wise* should be recognized as encompassing infinity. Schlegel does not refrain from interpreting Lessing's work altogether, however. He sees *Nathan the Wise* as a call for a new religion encompassing freedom, simplicity, nobility, and morality (187).

In the end, "Über Lessing" does not, as Schlegel promised, offer a complete characterization of Lessing and his work. The text remained

---

[3] "'Nathan' ist, wie mich dünkt, ein *Lessingisches* Gedicht; es ist *Lessings Lessing*, das *Werk schlechthin* unter seinen Werken, in dem vorher bestimmten Sinne; es ist die *Fortsetzung vom 'Anti-Goeze', Nummero zwölf*. Es ist unstreitig das eigenste, eigensinnigste und sonderbarste unter allen Lessingischen Produkten" (183).

unfinished for several years despite Schlegel's continued assurances that he would revise and conclude the piece. When he finally took the project up again in 1801 he admitted that he could not conclude the text in the same manner in which he had started it, and the text's new section is markedly different from the first (188). During the four years that passed between the writing of the two sections Schlegel's aesthetic and literary ideas changed considerably. Hans Eichner, in the introduction to the third volume of Behler's *Kritische Friedrich-Schlegel-Ausgabe*, calls 1801 a turning point for Schlegel (Behler 1975, III xiii). In fact, it is in the Lessing essay that Schlegel bids his readers "ein kritisches Lebewohl [a critical farewell]" and announces his resignation from any criticism for the future (190). Lessing no longer fits Schlegel's idea of a romantic poet, and therefore he reduces Lessing to the position of a mere forerunner of the romantic movement. Schlegel still expresses respect for Lessing, but he seems to have lost his former love and admiration. Lessing is no longer his "Leitstern [immortal guiding star]" (189; cf. Krüger 1913, 79; Wessels 1979, 163).

This shift in enthusiasm reflected a shift in Schlegel's conception of criticism. Whereas before, Schlegel believed that ideal criticism combined philosophy and poetry, he now calls for an "Enzyklopädie," a "science of art" that would provide "positive criticism" with objective laws (191). Any work that does not contribute to art and science or that does not relate to the development of genius simply does not exist for the "whole" and should therefore be ignored by this new criticism ("was fürs Ganze und im Ganzen eigentlich nicht existiert," 191). Schlegel bemoans the fact that this science of art does not yet exist.

If an "Enzyklopädie," and thus positive criticism, does not yet exist as Schlegel envisions it, what then is the significance of Lessing as a critic, according to Schlegel? Schlegel gives two reasons for his continued respect for Lessing. First he is still intrigued by the mixture of literature, polemic, wit, and philosophy in Lessing (189). But he adds a new thought: "Ich ehre Lessing wegen der *großen Tendenz* seines philosophischen Geistes und wegen der *symbolischen Form seiner Werke* [I respect Lessing because of the great tendency of his philosophical spirit and because of the symbolic form of his work]" (192). The changed use of the word "tendency" is interesting. As we have seen, in 1797 Schlegel warned critics not to reduce an infinite work like *Nathan the Wise* to a single cause, to a "trivial tendency" (1797, 186).[4] Now, however, the word loses all negative connotation. *Tendency* is infinite and

---

[4] The term *Tendenzdichtung* is also commonly used pejoratively in the nineteenth century to denote literature in pursuit of political aims.

progressive, referring to the "whole." In other words, works of art may have a certain objective, but only if they are expressions of true genius do they suggest a "tendency" as Schlegel understands the term. Tendency, then, is what relates the individual work to the "whole." What Schlegel means becomes clearer when one looks at his concept of "symbolic form." True art relates to the "whole,"[5] and the symbol helps the artist to make this connection. In the symbolic relationship, borders between art and nature are effaced. Whereas the philosophical work had been Schlegel's previous idea of the highest achievement, the symbolic work now took this position (1801, 194). Applying his new insight to Lessing's writing, Schlegel changed his list of favorite works. *Nathan the Wise* and the *Anti-Goeze* are replaced by *Ernst und Falk* and the *Erziehung des Menschengeschlechts* (195). These two texts are not only "symbolic" as Schlegel sees them, they are also fragmentary. The fragment is possibly the highest form of art in Schlegel's eyes. It is certainly the genre he preferred for his own writing. The question is whether he did Lessing justice by calling him a great writer of intimations and fragments. Without any obvious motivation, Schlegel inserted a collection of his own fragmentary writing ("Eisenfeile") into the text about Lessing, as if to demonstrate the type of literature he envisioned. That there was not enough of Lessing's work to illustrate his point proves that Schlegel promoted his own cause more than Lessing's. Thus he not only rendered his own unique interpretation of Lessing but he also misrepresented Lessing's work (cf. Höhle 1977, 126 and 132). This misrepresentation becomes even more obvious in Schlegel's next encounter with Lessing.

In 1804 three volumes of Lessing's work, assembled and edited by Schlegel, were published. They were titled *Lessings Gedanken und Meinungen aus dessen Schriften zusammengestellt und erläutert von Friedrich Schlegel* [Lessing's Thoughts and Opinions compiled from his Work and commented by Friedrich Schlegel]. The edition was dedicated to the Romantic philosopher Johann Gottlieb Fichte, whose idealism by this time impressed Schlegel more than Lessing's rationalism. *Nathan the Wise* was the only dramatic work that Schlegel included in the selections. It was also one of only three texts reprinted in their entirety without being shortened or rearranged. Thus, Schlegel once

---

[5] "Das Wesen der höhern Kunst und Form besteht in der *Beziehung aufs Ganze*" (193).

more made Lessing look like a writer of predominantly theoretical and fragmentary works.[6]

In the foreword, Schlegel confirms his view that Lessing is primarily to be considered a writer of criticism (Schlegel 1804, 51). Lessing lived at a time, Schlegel writes, when German literature was just experiencing a rebirth (after its first heyday in the Middle Ages) and when art was perceived as needing to be moved in new directions. This movement is exactly what Lessing achieved with his criticism, according to Schlegel. As Lessing himself moved toward the "good," never compromising himself by trying to appeal to the vulgar public, he motivated and inspired others to do the same (68). By his wit and his ease in combining different styles, he proved that he had the strength to think for himself. This strength — Schlegel calls it "Selbstdenken" — is the greatest lesson to be learnt from Lessing (84). Without him, German literature might not have reemerged from the deep sleep it had fallen into after the twelfth and thirteenth centuries (66). Schlegel concludes by saying that Lessing's position was not an easy one: he stood alone, upright, a fighter (70).[7]

Schlegel had expressed similar views previously. His interpretation, however, then takes a surprising, conservative and even mystical turn. When he characterizes Lessing as a prototypical Protestant, he does not just refer to Lessing's religious affiliation. In "Vom Character der Protestanten [Of the Character of Protestants]," the foreword to the third volume of *Lessings Gedanken und Meinungen* which contains *Nathan the Wise*, Schlegel describes how he sees the Christian religion. Protestantism postulates freedom of thought — which is good. On the other hand, Protestantism seems essentially a "negative" religion because it is polemical. It protests, as the name suggests, and will continue to do so until the end, when all of religion will have been protested against and the world will have been completely secularized (89). Catholicism, on the other hand, is an affirmative religion, which makes it a positive one in Schlegel's eyes (86). How did Lessing fit into this schema? Schlegel sees him as a polemical fighter, a Protestant, who, nevertheless, embraced "positivity" towards the end of his life. It is especially *Ernst und Falk* and *Erziehung des Menschengeschlechts* that lent themselves to Schlegel's interpretation of Lessing's "homecoming," a homecoming not to modern Catholicism but to the true Christian religion as it existed before the

---

[6] Probably because of the heavy emphasis on theoretical texts, Schlegel's Lessing edition was not very popular and hardly sold (Behler 1975, III xxxiii f.).

[7] Johanna Krüger hypothesizes that Schlegel describes here his own sense of isolation more than Lessing's conflicts (1913, 87).

Reformation. Lessing, Schlegel asserts, felt the need to reinstate positivity, thus he preached this new faith in his later works. He was the "Verkünder eines neuen Evangeliums [Proclaimer of a new Gospel]" (93).

Lessing's fatalistic and pantheistic ideas did not make sense in this perspective and Schlegel dismisses them as mistakes Lessing, if he had lived, would have eventually worked out (92). Obviously, this is a subjective interpretation that has more to do with Schlegel's own religious ideas (he converted to Catholicism in 1808) than with Lessing's. Margaret R. Higonnet is only one of the many critics who have expressed dissatisfaction with the "quasi-conversion of Lessing into a Catholic" (1979, 97); Heinz Härtl, another modern scholar who is taken aback by Schlegel's re-interpretation of Lessing, accuses him of perverting Lessing's position into its very opposite. Lessing did not want to return to mystic medieval Christianity, writes Härtl. He wanted to surpass Christian religion altogether (1984, 212). In addition to being a misinterpretation of Lessing's views, Schlegel's argument also contradicts his earlier thesis that Lessing stayed loyal to one great "tendency" in his life. Other critics describe Lessing as a profound Christian thinker, but few go as far as Schlegel who turns him into a mystical evangelist.

Schlegel's Lessing interpretation was of paramount importance in shaping a certain image of Lessing that in part still survives. This image derives more from Schlegel's earlier essays than from his later ones. Essentially, Schlegel introduced the notion that Lessing needs to be respected primarily for his ground-breaking work as a critic and philosopher. Even though some deplored the lack of warmth and poetic genius in Lessing's dramas before, few dared to argue against this point once Schlegel presented it as *fait accompli*.[8] Schlegel also initiated an intense preoccupation with Lessing's character. He paved the way for the nationalization and idealization of Lessing that was to follow (cf. Barner *et al.* [5]1987, 392).[9]

---

[8] Among Schlegel's contemporaries who insist that Lessing's plays are poetic works are Adam Müller (1806) and Friedrich Bouterwek (1819).

[9] Anita Liepert, a former East German critic, considers Schlegel the initiator of the apologetic bourgeois interpretation of Lessing, while "research proper" did not start until Heinrich Heine picked up the topic of Lessing in the 1830s (1971, 1321).

b: Schiller

Considering that Lessing today is often called one of the three major German writers, along with Friedrich Schiller and Johann Wolfgang von Goethe, and that they were separated by only a generation, it is a little surprising to find that the two Classicists themselves did not have much to say about Lessing. Lessing lived to see the public successes of their early dramas, as well as Goethe's seminal *Leiden des jungen Werther* [Sorrows of Young Werther]. Lessing was still considered the grand master of German literature at the time. Looking back on his early years in his autobiography *Dichtung und Wahrheit* [Poetry and Truth], Goethe recalled the effect Lessing and especially *Emilia Galotti* had had on him as a young person. But when he had the opportunity to actually meet Lessing — Goethe was a student in the town of Leipzig in the late 1760s and Lessing happened to be passing through — he passed up the chance out of a sense of false pride (Goethe 1811, 233). Nor did Lessing ever make an effort to come into contact with Goethe or Schiller. His attitude toward both writers was one of reserved respect. Many years after the Leipzig incident, Goethe finally decided to visit Lessing, but the plan was thwarted by Lessing's death.

Lessing had a certain influence on the young Schiller that can be easily seen in Schiller's early theoretical writing and especially in *Don Carlos*. Later, however, Schiller moved away from Lessing's model. The classic drama created by Goethe and Schiller, with its elevated form and ideal content, was quite different from Lessing's plays. Only *Nathan the Wise*, with its Humanist concerns and verse form, came close to the "sublime" style of classical writing. Even *Nathan the Wise*, however, did not completely satisfy Schiller's expectations (cf. Albrecht 1984 on Schiller's ambivalent relationship to Lessing, 220). While Schiller defends the play in 1783, he finds fault, typically, with its coldness in *Über naive und sentimentalische Dichtung* [Of naive and sentimental poetry] (1795, 446). He criticizes the drama for not being a true tragedy and maintains that it might just as easily be transformed into a comedy.

Despite his objections, Schiller prepared a version of *Nathan the Wise* that was to be staged by Goethe on the renowned Weimar stage in 1801 (Schiller 1801). This production was a breakthrough as far as the play's acceptance into the German theatrical repertory was concerned. Schiller made the play digestible to the viewer by cutting about one fourth of the dialogue and deleting many of the lengthy didactic or polemical passages. Some verses, especially the ones containing "prosaic" expressions and references to money, as well as "oriental" clues were either altered or deleted. Thus, Schiller emphasized the ideal aspects of the play, elevating it onto a more abstract level than Lessing had intended. On the other hand, the changes were not as dramatic as sometimes assumed (cf. Demetz 1971, 739f.), and Wessels recognizes Schiller's effort to leave intact the content and style of the original (1979, 261). Schiller also resisted the temptation to turn Nathan into a tragic hero and retained him as a basically "bourgeois" character (Wessels 1979, 272).

The immediate reaction to the production was favorable, and the play began to be performed — despite Lessing's own gloomy prediction that *Nathan the Wise* might never be performed onstage (Lessing 1970-1979, II 723). Throughout the nineteenth century the play was well established in German theatrical repertories. Ludwig Tieck even goes so far as to say that there was no small city or village pub that did not pride itself on offering the play as entertainment for the learned population (1825, 231). In some cities, however, the play had trouble getting past the censor because of its alleged anti-Christian attitude. In Vienna, for example, it could not be produced until 1819. *Nathan the Wise* was finally accepted as a "classic" drama when it had conquered the German stage. Sixty years after Schiller's production David Friedrich Strauß could write: "der 'Nathan' hat sich auch als ein höchst wirksames Bühnenstück bewährt [*Nathan* has proven itself on stage as a highly effective play]" (1861, 44).

3: The Nineteenth Century

a: The Historical School

WHILE CLASSICISM SET THE standard for literature and art in the nineteenth century, a new theory also emerged that tried to describe and perhaps even create aesthetic criteria of its own. At the same time that "high" literature established itself as an altogether different entity from less sophisticated writing, a systematic theoretical approach replaced the previously random criticism and literary reviews. Historians today speak of the beginning of "Literaturwissenschaft," or literary studies. Three major phases of this development can be distinguished: the historical approach, Positivism, and "Geistesgeschichte." The three names associated with these phases are Georg Gottfried Gervinus, Wilhelm Dilthey, and Wilhelm Scherer.

Georg Gottfried Gervinus was one of the seven Göttingen professors who in 1837 accused Ernst August, King of Hannover, of violating the constitution and were consequently dismissed from their university posts and exiled. He was primarily a historian and was only marginally interested in literary studies. Literature served him mainly to illustrate his theory of society's dialectical progress toward a political state of freedom and unity. His theory was clearly inspired by Hegel's (cf. Hohendahl 1985a, 175-187). It expressed the pre-1848 optimism and hope of the liberal bourgeoisie (March 1848 marks the date of the failed revolution in France and Germany — thus the term *Vormärz* [Pre-March] for the literary period preceding this event).[1] Gervinus's *Neuere Geschichte der poetischen National-Literatur der Deutschen* [New History of the National Poetic Literature of Germany] was published in 1840. Here, Lessing appears as the figure who returned literature to its German origins, who wrote in the natural German idiom and described true human beings (1840, 319). At the same time, Lessing is hailed as "das eigentliche Revolutionsgenie [the true genius of revolution]" (321) who had no other principle than to have no principle. As did Friedrich Schlegel before him, Gervinus recognizes Lessing's merit in the way he advised readers to search for their own paths in life. Gervinus interprets this advice as a political act. Schlegel, on the other hand, had less interest in politics and neglected this aspect of

---

[1] The revolution of 1848 lends itself as a date of division, even if critics such as Hohendahl warn their readers not to overestimate the influence of the year and its political events (1985a, 130 and 158).

Lessing's writing when describing the ideal, all-encompassing "Enzyklopä-die." Gervinus is quite specific in connecting Lessing's revolutionary spirit to liberal ideals:

> Es ist die ewige Opposition gegen den faulen Schlendrian der deutschen Kleinmeisterei und die Armseligkeit des deutschen Gelehr-tenlebens, das fortwährende Ringen eines liberalen Geistes gegen die vielfachen Beschränkungen der materiellen Welt [It is the never ending opposition to the lazy dawdling of German tediousness and to the wretchedness of the life of German intellectuals, the continuous struggle of a liberal mind against the numerous limitations of the material world]" (322).

Gervinus considered *Nathan the Wise* not only to be Lessing's legacy but also to be the most peculiar and most German work next to Goethe's *Faust* (413). The nation should absorb this work and its morality, he believed, much more profoundly than it already had. Gervinus then graciously excuses the drama's "bad verses" (413).

Heinrich Heine shared with Gervinus and other representatives of the historical school[2] an interest in the relationship between literature and politics. Lessing was especially popular among this group of intellectuals (cf. Lecke 1980, 147). In his theoretical work *Die romantische Schule* [The Romantic School] (1836), Heine writes respectfully: "Mehr als man ahnte, war Lessing auch politisch bewegt, eine Eigenschaft, die wir bei seinen Zeitgenossen gar nicht finden... [More than generally assumed, Lessing possessed political motivation, a trait not easily found among his contemporaries" (260). Lessing was the author of literary history whom Heine loved best (261). Heine was also never able to resist a pun, and so he especially appreciated Lessing's style and wit, as he writes in *Zur Geschichte der Religion und Philosophie in Deutschland* [On the History of Religion and Philosophy in Germany] (1835): "sein Witz war vielmehr ein großer deutscher Kater, der mit der Maus spielt, ehe er sie würgt [his wit was a big German cat who plays with the mouse before strangling it]" (262). His love and respect stemmed, however, more from sympathy with the man than from admiration for his literature. Heine admits that the philosophical and theological disputes are more important to him than Lessing's dramas (264). What he says about Lessing's tragic fate —

---

[2] Heine is mainly known as a representative of "Junges Deutschland [Young Germany]," a school associated with such political writers as Ludwig Börne and Karl Gutzkow. The "Jungdeutsch" and left-wing Hegelian viewpoints are to be distinguished (cf. Hohendahl 1985a, 146). Nevertheless, Heine, Gervinus, Ruge, and others are here summarized under the heading of "historical school," since their approach to Lessing shares general aspects.

he mentions his loneliness and isolation, his steadfastness and honesty, his unhappiness and his genius — is not original.

Heine becomes somewhat mystical when he declares Luther and Lessing to be the two liberators of Germany who would soon be succeeded by the much-awaited "third man" in golden armor.[3] Whether this comment is meant to be taken ironically or whether Heine actually wanted to foretell Germany's religious and political liberation is not clear. Such "romantic" aspects of Heine's and also Gervinus's interpretations have led Wilfried Barner and his co-editors of *Lessing: Epoche — Werk — Wirkung* (1987) to pose the question whether they did not involuntarily pander to the "nationalization" of Lessing by the Prussian historiographers (397f.). Heine's assessment of *Nathan the Wise* was also not very profound. He is treading on safe ground when he calls the play a "philosophical-theological treatise in favor of pure Deism" (1835, 264) — one might have expected a deeper understanding from Heine.

Another writer of the "Vormärz" was Arnold Ruge, who belonged to the so-called Linkshegelianer [left-wing Hegelians]. This group believed in the dialectical principle suggested by Hegel and applied his theory to politics. Like Schlegel before and Mehring after him, Ruge was completely dismayed by previous Lessing criticism (1847, 19). In his *Geschichte der deutschen Poesie und Philosophie seit Lessing* [History of German Poetry and Philosophy since Lessing], he interprets literature as an expression of *Zeitgeist*. It has little subjective or symbolic meaning. To Ruge, Lessing represents the German Enlightenment in its deepest and purest form (20). He not only expressed the aesthetic, the religious, and the universal consciousness of his time but he could have even functioned as the political spokesperson for his era, writes Ruge. What kept him from entering the political arena was disappointment about his disinterested contemporaries, Ruge hypothesizes (20). As did so many other thinkers from different periods and ideological schools, Ruge revered Lessing as the pioneer who paved the way for political progress that was to come after his death. He was a pioneer even though some of his ideas have become "antiquated" — Ruge is thinking of Lessing's preference for the fable: Lessing wrote many *Fabeln* in Aesop's style, and he also used a fable in *Nathan the Wise*. Despite this negative criticism, *Nathan the Wise* fares well with Ruge. He interprets the play in a rather traditional manner, focusing on the ideal of "Humanität" and refraining from an outright political analysis.

---

[3] "Ja, kommen wird auch der dritte Mann, der da vollbringt, was Luther begonnen, was Lessing fortgesetzt, und dessen das deutsche Vaterland so sehr bedarf, — der dritte Befreier! — Ich sehe schon seine goldne Rüstung, die aus dem purpurnen Kaisermantel hervorstrahlt, 'wie die Sonne aus dem Morgenrot!'" (1835, 262)

Several years after the revolution of 1848 Ferdinand Lassalle, founder of the Social Democratic movement, still adhered to the liberal principles of the Vormärz. His essay "Gotthold Ephraim Lessing," written in 1858 and published in 1861, picks up from Heine's comparison of Lessing to Luther. Taking it one step further, Lassalle calls Lessing "The Greater Luther," greater because he was not handicapped by religious interests (165). Lassalle looks at Lessing from a cultural-historical viewpoint that admitted political aspects as well. The one play that most qualifies as a political one in his eyes is *Minna von Barnhelm* (166). This appreciation has to do with Lassalle's estimation of Lessing and Frederick the Great (king of Prussia from 1740 to 1786) as the monumental revolutionaries of their time. It did not occur to Lassalle that any references to Frederick that Lessing made in *Minna* might have been intended to criticize the Prussian king. At this point, Lassalle's interpretation corresponds to the nineteenth century bourgeois German standpoint, which took Frederick the Great as its hero. Adolf Stahr especially promoted this view. In 1859 he published a biography of Lessing that became extremely popular, in which he portrays Lessing as a "republican" who thought no less of himself than did the great Prussian king (Stahr 1859, 339). Lassalle praises Stahr's biography as the only one of worth (186) and takes his cue from it. Lessing, Lassalle writes, was a revolutionary in the realm of the intellect as Frederick was in the realm of politics (164). The characters of *Nathan the Wise*, for example, are the realization of bourgeois ideals such as individuality and self-confidence (167f.). Their progress toward their individual perfection impresses Lassalle as a dialectical principle. He then points to the "soldier-heroes" Tellheim and Odoardo in the plays *Minna von Barnhelm* and *Emilia Galotti*. Soldiers, according to Lassalle, are the ultimate realization of Lessing's ideal independent personality.

This interpretation rests on the assumption that Tellheim and Odoardo are positive heros. Many more recent critics see both characters in a less positive light and argue that Tellheim and Odoardo are best understood as tragic figures holding on to false ideas. Lassalle seems to sense that Lessing's plays do not make complete sense from his viewpoint, and that is why he is quick to refer to Hegel. Lassalle, as well as Gervinus and Ruge, commend Hegel as the person who translated Lessing's individualized notion of a progressive development into a more general and historical frame (176f.).

Wolfgang Menzel, who published the second edition of his *Die deutsche Literatur* [German Literature] in 1836, also took a historical perspective in his literary criticism. His results, however, are quite different from Heine's or Gervinus's. While Menzel in his youth had been one of the founders of the politically progressive students' associations of the late 1810s, he later became one of the most radical opponents of Vormärz, the literary school that favored democratic reforms. In fact, the ban on "Young-German" literature pronounced in 1835 was partly caused by Menzel's attacks on writers such as Gutzkow and Heine. Menzel's viewpoint was dominated by his nationalism. In *Die deutsche Literatur* he applauds Lessing for his fight against the French, Greek, and English "craze" (Menzel [2]1836, 276). Menzel thus hits upon a theme that reappears in Lessing interpretation for years to come. He depicts Lessing as a free and independent writer who might have rescued Germany from all the foreign influences had Goethe and Classicism not led literature into "the soft mud of sentimentality and affectation" (277). Whereas Goethe represents effeminacy, Lessing stands proud as a true "man." Surprisingly, the conservative Menzel does not attack the humanism of *Nathan the Wise* in any way and understands Lessing's motivation for writing the play as a reaction to the intolerance Lessing's Jewish friend, the "liebenswürdige Mendelssohn [lovable Mendelssohn]," had had to endure (280f.). *Nathan the Wise* is presented as an exemplary work, a natural and unpretentious poem expressing the "sweetest wisdom" (280f.). Its iambic verse is praised as an achievement never duplicated. Menzel, however, does not say a word about the content of the play.

Heinrich von Treitschke, an enthusiastic Prussian patriot, admired in Lessing, as did Gervinus and Heine, someone whose deeds had political significance for years to come (376f.). Nevertheless, in his essay "Lessing" (1863) Treitschke regrets a certain limitation in Lessing's political understanding. He speaks of "eine Lücke in der Bildung [a gap in Lessing's education]" (377). This supposed gap is visible in Lessing's inability to understand patriotism as well as in his lack of approval for the Prussian state (378). Treitschke finds it particularly tragic that Lessing did not recognize in Frederick the Great the founder of the modern state (380). As we will see later (pp. 46-48), this interpretation provoked a response from Franz Mehring, who felt contempt for Frederick and the Prussian qualities he represented. In his *Lessing-Legende* (1893), Mehring attacks the attempts of writers such as Adolf Stahr and Heinrich von Treitschke to mold Lessing into a "Prussian in disguise" and put him on a pedestal next to Frederick the Great.

b: Positivism

By the middle of the century another school of criticism emerged: Positivism. Its major representative, Wilhelm Scherer, was interested in history merely as a source for "positive" — factual — information, gathered in an almost scientific manner. As apolitical as this approach pretended to be, conservative values were hidden in it. At best, the refusal to get involved in political affairs must be interpreted as a silent acceptance of the status quo.

Theodor Danzel, one of Positivism's first practitioners, published the first volume of his Lessing biography in 1849. He had gathered an impressive amount of background information, anecdotes, quotes, and documents. After Danzel's death the second volume (1854) was finished by G.E. Guhrauer. There is little new insight into Lessing's writing. On *Nathan the Wise*, the authors take a defensive stand. While they protest against the overemphasis of many critics on Lessing's critical abilities at the price of denying him poetic talent (II 106f.), they only gesture toward acknowledging poetic elements in *Nathan the Wise*. There is as much poetry in it as Lessing was capable of, they say.

The authors also take a stand against accusations that focus on Lessing's alleged defamation of Christianity. Does not the simple Templar fulfill Jesus's ideal? they ask (202f.). And does the love and self-abnegation demanded in the ring parable not describe Christianity? Obviously, the theological dispute over *Nathan the Wise* was still on the mind of nineteenth century critics, and they felt the need to defend Lessing against the orthodox position.

W. von Maltzahn and R. Boxberger, the editors of the 1880-1881 revised version of the Danzel's biography (Guhrauer died shortly after finishing the second volume), kept up the apologetic tone. In some instances, they try to slightly shift the focus. Danzel's hypothesis that *Nathan the Wise* was intended to be a glorification of Christianity (II 465), for example, is weighed against Nathan's position, which is taken as Lessing's own. The editors expect any serious theologian of their century to agree with Nathan and his philosophy (478). Since the book is a biography rather than a critical work on Lessing's writing, a lot of biographical information comes out in the discussions of the plays. Maltzahn and Boxberger recognize some of Malchen König, Lessing's stepdaughter, in Recha (475). They also point to the impact that East Indian philosophy had on *Nathan the Wise* (471). All the factual information, however, does not hide the ideological basis of the work. Lassalle had seen in Lessing a representative of bourgeois ideology. Maltzahn and Boxberger see him that way also, only their values are politically conservative. To Lassalle, Lessing was a political revolutionary; for Maltzahn and Boxberger, he is one of Germany's great Humanists, along with Goethe and Schiller (497f.).

The Positivist par excellence, Wilhelm Scherer, wrote about Lessing several times. His thinking is dialectical and presumes that any good idea will prevail in the end. In his essay "Zu Lessings 'Nathan'" (1870) he affirms that

Nathan the Wise contains such a good idea — humanism (328). Scherer claims that humanism was first "planted" in European culture in the thirteenth century, and that it was passed down through the generations to Lessing's open and tolerant grandfather Theophilus Lessing and then to Gotthold Ephraim, who presented the idea to his readers. Lessing was thus the final step in the development of human progress.

The notion that Lessing was connecting various threads of tradition and history reappears in a later text by Scherer, "Gotthold Ephraim Lessing. Zum 15. Februar 1881" (Scherer 1881). His thesis is that Lessing began work on *Nathan the Wise* around 1750. Lessing's *Alcibiades* and *The Jews* were preliminary studies (62f.), Scherer writes. Lessing was also greatly influenced by Voltaire. Scherer takes for fact Karl Lessing's allegation that the famous French writer and philosopher Voltaire and the young translator Lessing were acquainted. Not only Voltaire's studies of Islamic history and Saladin are said to have influenced Lessing, but also Voltaire's play of 1751, *Amélie ou le Dux de Foix* (67). Scherer's paper may not be a seminal work on *Nathan the Wise*, but it is an early attempt at the type of literary criticism that is concerned with uncovering historical sources and creative processes.

c: Geistesgeschichte

After positivism comes "Geistesgeschichte," an interpretive approach interested primarily in "great art" created by "great men." It gives up the pseudo-scientific, "objective" stand of earlier schools. Literature is combed for proof of its morality and harmony, the two characteristics said to prevail in humanity, society, and the universe. Nowhere is art considered more perfected than in Classicism. The Enlightenment is thus pushed into the background and given credit only for laying the groundwork for a developing morality and for the ripening self-consciousness of the bourgeois class. Lessing is especially revered as a pioneer in matters of morality and humanism.

Joseph von Eichendorff's interpretation of Lessing is reminiscent of but less sophisticated than Schlegel's earlier analysis. He does not fit well into any larger school of thought. His views are Christian-conservative, usually classified as "late Romantic." In several major poetic studies (*Der deutsche Roman des achtzehnten Jahrhunderts in seinem Verhältniß zum Christenthum* [The German Novel of the Eighteenth Century in its Relation to Christianity], 1851, *Zur Geschichte des Dramas* [On the History of Drama], 1854, and *Geschichte der poetischen Literatur Deutschlands* [History of Germany's poetic Literature], 1857), Eichendorff demands that art should relate to Christian thought (1854, 421). He recognizes Lessing as one of the first writers to make the topic of religion literally acceptable in Germany (1854, 399). As Schlegel did before him, Eichendorff describes Lessing as a Protestant who carried his Protestantism to extremes, but he denies that this was done in pure "negation" (1851, 111). Rather, Eichendorff pictures Lessing as driven by doubt. Because Lessing never achieved peace or salvation, because he perished, like Moses, without having found the "Promised Land," Eichendorff pities him as the most tragic character of German literature (1851, 109; 1857, 227). He understands the publication of Reimarus's *Fragments* as Lessing's attempt to mend the split between orthodox and freethinking Protestants. Lessing wanted the *Fragments* contradicted and proven wrong, Eichendorff claims (1854, 353). This is not what happened, however, and Lessing died without satisfying his search for the "new Gospel," Eichendorff adds regretfully. Disagreeing with Schlegel's views described above, Eichendorff does not seem to think Lessing could have ever found what he was looking for.

Eichendorff is also only in superficial accord with Schlegel when it comes to appreciating Lessing's poetic qualities. While Schlegel called *Emilia Galotti* an example of "dramatic algebra," Eichendorff employs the metaphor of a chess game ("ein tief durchdachtes Schachspiel [a deeply thought through game of chess]," 1857, 241). Schlegel attested to Lessing's poetic genius in his philosophical work, but Eichendorff objects to Lessing's insistence on reason. Poetry, in his mind, is "etwas [something]" that goes beyond reason (1857, 240). What the "etwas" is that makes a poet a poet and that Lessing lacked, Eichendorff cannot really say. *Nathan the Wise*, he writes, could have been a masterpiece, but it is too polemical, and it unfairly pushes Christianity into the background (1857, 252). The humanism that Lessing wishes to promote in his last play is, argues Eichendorff, an alternative religion, a religion that replaces God with reason — something Eichendorff, a staunch Catholic, could not condone.

David Friedrich Strauß deals with theological aspects of the drama. In 1835-1836 he upset his superiors and his German readers by dismissing the Gospels as myths in his famous book *Das Leben Jesu, kritisch bearbeitet* [The Life of Jesus, critically examined]. As a result, he was fired from his position as professor in Tübingen. His last work, *Der alte und der neue Glaube* [Old and New Faith] (1872) proposed a new religion to replace Christianity that would incorporate the findings of modern science and evolutionary theory. Because his vision of a perfect society entails humanism combined with true (i.e., undogmatic) religion, he approves of Lessing's attack on dogma and the church in *Nathan the Wise* (1861, 34). The humanism he recognizes in the play is of an ideal nature, which renders all concrete aspects incidental. Accordingly, Strauß considers Nathan's Jewishness irrelevant (32).

Friedrich Theodor Vischer, in his *Ästhetik oder Wissenschaft des Schönen* [Aesthetics or Science of the Beautiful] (1846-1857), criticized *Nathan the Wise* for its "happy end," which he saw as compromising the serious character of the drama (327). The final scene, he found, was no better than the end to any family play. Like most nineteenth century theorists, Vischer favored tragedy as the "truer, deeper, and more meaningful form" of drama (326). Strauß, however, disagrees with Vischer. He defends the sentimental ending of *Nathan the Wise* as a necessary element of the play's ideal message, which was that delusion will ultimately be conquered by reason (Strauß 1861, 43). While the fact that the play has a message makes it a "didactic drama," Strauß is quick to point out that didactic literature need not lack poetic value. *Nathan the Wise*, especially, Strauß concludes, is "eine Perle der Dichtung [a poetic gem]" (43).

In his *Lessing-Studien* (1862) C. Hebler vehemently contests the idea that Lessing wanted to raise Judaism above Christianity. In *Nathan the Wise*, Hebler argues, true religion makes all three positive religions (Judaism, Islam, and Christianity) look equally inferior. Only in the *Erziehung des Menschengeschlechts* (*The Education of the Human Race*, translated in Lessing 1991), the work in which Lessing actually compares the positive religions, can Hebler identify a preference for the Christian religion (17). Lessing could not have been a Deist, Hebler concludes, or else he would not have validated positive religion as a step on the path to true rational religion (20).

In his lecture "Studien zu Lessings Nathan" (1865), Ernst Köpke resurrected some of the arguments that Tralles had used one hundred years earlier in his crude attack on Lessing. To put the three religions on the same level seems particularly offensive to Köpke (33). The Christian religion is better than all others. No one can be a true "man" without first being a Christian. Lessing's major fault, says Köpke, is that he assumes love to be a substantial part of all religions, when it really belongs to Christianity alone (37). From a literary perspective, the play does not come off any better. Köpke finds plenty to complain of: the story is too complex and is presented in a confusing way, the characters do not provoke any human sympathy, Nathan is a "cowardly schemer," the verses do not "flow," and Lessing was actually not a poet at all (10ff.). In an earlier essay, "Über 'Nathan den Weisen'" (1856), Köpke had noted that *Nathan the Wise* was particularly unsuited for instruction in school because it taught young minds to doubt rather than to have faith (cf. von König 1974, on banning *Nathan the Wise* from school education). All the more happy is Köpke in his later lecture to find that critics have taken the play — against its original intention — to be a testimony of love advancing the cause of Christianity (39).

Wilhelm Dilthey, the major representative of "Geistesgeschichte," wanted to "understand" the work of art, to find its subjective meaning. Through art, he thought, the meaning of life would reveal itself. He was also a strong believer in Classicism. In "Die Weltanschauung Lessings [The Philosophy of Lessing]" (1867) he busily draws parallels to Goethe, Schiller, and Beethoven. The terms he uses to analyze *Nathan the Wise*, such as "Seelengröße [greatness of soul]" (46) and "verklärte Heiterkeit [radiant serenity]" (48) immediately evoke such a relationship. Dilthey values *Nathan the Wise* as a forerunner of Goethe's "Seelendrama" (59). Also, he notes, the play established the iambic meter as that of Germany's dramatic verse (61). When Dilthey is not occupied with formal aspects of the play, he describes its "meaning" by using such abstract terms as *beauty, serenity*, and *gentleness* (53). Missing in this analysis is any reference to a concrete or historical circumstance. How does Dilthey conceptualize "love of humanity" in a society? Does he think of Germany at all when he projects the vision of a harmonious community independent of nation, class, or confession? Would he object to Nathan's central position in the play (60) if Nathan was not a Jew? The idea that individuals can dissociate from their social and national identities, which are often part of an unpleasant and frustrating reality, is a dream characteristic of the bourgeoisie in the late nineteenth century. Reduced to this perspective, *Nathan the Wise* serves as utopia where free spirits liberate themselves from society and content themselves with thoughts of their "humanity" (54).

Kuno Fischer shares some of Köpke's views in his *G.E. Lessing als Reformator der deutschen Literatur* [G.E. Lessing as Reformer of German Literature] ([3]1881). Köpke and Fischer agree, for example, that the characters in *Nathan the Wise* were not true representatives of their respective religions. Yet Fischer's motivation is quite different from Köpke's. Helmut Göbel is wrong to accuse Fischer in the commentary to a paperback edition of *Nathan the Wise* (1977, 258f.) of anticipating later forms of anti-Semitism. Göbel should have chosen Köpke's text to make this point. This is not to say that Fischer's liberal perspective, or any idealistic and liberal perspective, is immune to prejudice and racism. While Köpke firmly believed in the superiority of Christianity, however, Fischer rebuked those who felt that Lessing attacked Christianity. Resorting to Lessing's *Erziehung des Menschengeschlechts*, the "key" to understanding *Nathan the Wise*, Fischer concludes that the three positive religions in question are merely stages on the path to an ideal state of true religion (1881, 70). In *Nathan the Wise*, Lessing wanted to compare the imperfect to the ideal state, intolerance and fanaticism to tolerance (36). Fischer writes that the Patriarch, for example, is not even close to having a true religion (93). The most oppressed peoples and races, on the other hand, can be "human" in the highest sense (this passage was the reason for Göbel's mistrust of its author). Fischer cannot, however, overlook the fact that Lessing did not bring society any closer to this goal of tolerance. He ends his book on a note that is typical of the optimism — or the resignation — of the liberal viewpoint: the day will come when the goal can be attained, though this day may not come soon.

In summary, it can be said that the rising bourgeoisie of the "Vor-" and "Nachmärz" period used Lessing for purposes of identification. More than any other of his works, *Nathan the Wise* was revered as a play that supplied this self-confident class with its values and principles.[4] That not only the German middle class but also the Jewish population drew from the play a sense of hope and emancipation will be discussed in the next chapter.

---

[4] Some critics disagree. Ludwig Tieck thinks most highly of *Minna von Barnhelm* (1855, 313). Friedrich Hebbel finds all of Lessing's plays detestable (1841). A few writers condemn *Nathan the Wise* on formal grounds. Otto Ludwig complains that the "snappy" style of the drama inflicts physical pain on its viewers. *Nathan the Wise* was taught in German schools (cf. Gast 1898; Herrlitz 1964), but *Minna von Barnhelm* was generally considered more suitable for students (cf. Barner et al. [5]1987, 278).

4: 1879 and 1881: Lessing and the Jews

THE "JEWISH" QUESTION is one inherently associated with *Nathan the Wise*. It has been discussed, from different angles, from the time of the first reviews. By the latter half of the nineteenth century two opposed positions crystallized. On the one hand, Jewish liberals had long referred to Lessing and especially to *Nathan the Wise* in support of Jewish emancipation. On the other hand, the anti-Semitic right began their attacks by also referring to Lessing.

A distinction between the religious and the political aspect of the "Jewish" question had been made earlier in the century — by Herder, for example, in his "Bekehrung der Juden [Conversion of the Jews]" (1802, 63). In this essay, Herder demonstrates that he understands and even supports the Jews' desire to preserve their unique ethnic and religious identity. But at the same time, he is concerned for his German compatriots and wonders how many Jews should be allowed to stay within German borders (64).[1] This passage was written just as Jews were slowly beginning their ascent into the middle and sometimes even the upper classes. Intellectuals and aristocrats approved of this movement and gathered in the salons of Jewish women such as Rahel Varnhagen. The Napoleonic era brought with it the "Judenedikt" (March 1812) and the passage of other civil rights legislation (cf. Holeczek 1982, 149). Only Jews with a special passport ("Schutzbrief") enjoyed these privileges, however (Schoeps 1977, 91), and after 1815 the situation worsened again. Obtaining jobs in universities or in the government was forbidden until 1871. The only way for a Jew to bypass the restrictions was to convert, an act of assimilation recommended by David Friedländer as early as 1799. Friedländer was not only a friend of Moses Mendelssohn but he was also the first (non-paid) Jewish member of the city council of Berlin. As a writer, he promoted Jewish emancipation. As the century progressed, intellectuals and aristocrats who had temporarily fraternized with Jews turned their backs. The aristocracy was offended when Jews started to climb up the social ladder in greater numbers (cf. Arendt [8]1990, 170). In the literary sphere, as romanticism turned conservative, men such as Achim von Arnim and Clemens Brentano, the founders of the "Christlich-Deutsche Tischgesellschaft [Christian-German

---

[1] Paul Lawrence Rose notices that "numerous anti-Jewish statements" in Herders writing remain unexplained (1990, 97).

Table Company]," also voiced anti-Jewish reservations. In 1869 Jews won a small victory when the Prussian king Wilhelm annulled all laws that differentiated between religions. Anti-Jewish sentiments among the population, however, escalated. The reason for the hatred of Jews was expressed no longer in religious terms but increasingly in terms of nationalism (cf. Boehlich 1965, 251; Grimm 1975, 168), notably by the conservative historian Heinrich von Treitschke. Treitschke, renowned for his antiliberal positions, published various articles and open letters between 1879 and 1881 that provoked what Walter Boehlich calls the "Berliner Antisemitismusstreit," a public dispute on the topic of anti-Semitism (1965). It was Treitschke who said the fateful words: "Die Juden sind unser Unglück [the Jews are our Misfortune]." In 1880 an anti-Semitic petition demanding the exclusion of Jews from public positions was delivered to Bismarck, carrying 250,000 signatures (cf. Fritsch [38]1935, 14 and 525; Boehlich 1965, 255). In protest, seventy-five distinguished personalities signed a counter-petition (reprinted in Boehlich 1965, 202-204). Walter Jens relates how the deputy Hänel spoke up in 1880 in parliament against anti-Jewish sentiment but only reaped laughter when he backed up his demand by calling on Lessing's *Nathan the Wise* (1982, 38f.). In 1893 the anti-Semites received a quarter of a million votes (cf. Boehlich 1965, 262).

a: Jewish Critics

As suggested earlier, Jews had felt obliged to Lessing even when they did not yet have a voice or a medium to express their esteem. It was only in the course of the nineteenth century that Jewish writers entered the literary arena. There were those who referred to Lessing as the guarantor and spokesperson for Jewish emancipation, but Guthke identifies another group that was more critical of Lessing: the Zionists (1975, 233f.). Especially by the later part of the century, Zionists felt that Lessing had promoted assimilation, which in the long run hampers the Jewish cause. In our time, Hans Mayer has defended a similar position by drawing a parallel between assimilation, as promoted by Lessing, and Auschwitz (pp. 64f.).

Before 1879, however, the opinions were almost completely unified in Lessing's favor. Gabriel Rießer reminds his fellow Israelites in a speech in 1838 of their indebtedness to Lessing (257). Lessing is an inspiration and an idol for Rießer (271, 281f.). In retrospect, he says, *Nathan the Wise* even gives meaning to the centuries of suffering Jews had to endure. Jews, Rießer suggests, can learn from Nathan's acceptance of fate and his willing consent not to revolt against Providence. In the end, one will even gain satisfaction and happiness by serving the humanistic ideas outlined in *Nathan the Wise*, concludes Rießer (279f.).

In 1860 a Lessing memorial was unveiled in Leipzig. Abraham Meyer Goldschmidt's lecture on the occasion expressed a similar reverence for Lessing. Goldschmidt goes a step farther than Rießer — that is, if the move from humanist to nationalist ideals can be called a progression: he expresses an optimistic and at the same time conservative attitude when he declares *Nathan the Wise* a historical deed that presented the Jews of Germany with a fatherland (346f.). He hopes that Germans and Jews can live together in friendship, following the example of Lessing and Moses Mendelssohn. Goldschmidt obviously needs to believe that prejudice and racism have been conquered and that the German nation has absorbed and embraced the idea of Jewish freedom and acceptance.

Abraham Geiger is more careful and much more realistic in his perception of historic circumstances (1862). He reminds his Jewish listeners that they still are a minority in Germany and depend on their instinct for self-preservation. The intellect, Geiger suggests, is especially important in this regard. Consequently, he emphasizes not Nathan's acceptance of Providence but rather the significance of reason in *Nathan the Wise*.

The years between 1879 and 1881 were particularly significant for German-Jewish relations. There were three commemorations in 1879 alone: Lessing and Moses Mendelssohn were honored on their 150th birthdays, and the 100th anniversary of *Nathan the Wise* was celebrated. A special publication by the Deutsch-Israelitischer Gemeindebund, the *Lessing-Mendelssohn Gedenkbuch*, is a collection of articles on the topics of the three celebrations. Berthold Auerbach, the best known of the contributors to the *Gedenkbuch*, deals with *Nathan the Wise* (1879). He concentrates on the ring parable and the significance it has for the play. In particular, he is interested in the judge's sentence, which implies that the three rings of the story are false. Likewise, the positive religions in question lack universal validity, interprets Auerbach. Judaism, Islam, and Christianity may contain humanistic values but they are not identical with humanism proper. What counts, therefore, is the humanity and religion that any one individual feels. Auerbach concludes his essay by hypothesizing about the *Derwisch*, a play Lessing intended to write but never did. Had he only finished it, Auerbach suggests, Lessing might have elaborated in more detail how religion is the responsibility of the individual's conscience.

A different concern is expressed by Aug. Wünsche in the same publication. His essay also deals with the parable, but Wünsche concentrates on the story's various medieval sources. Whereas most scholars point to Boccaccio as the source for Lessing's parable, Wünsche holds that a Jewish parable from 1480, written by Schebet Jehuda, could be considered the original version of the story. He admits, however, that Lessing might not have known this text, since he was obviously influenced by later versions of the parable where the question of which religion is the best was more important than in the earlier ones.

Arnold Bodek, in yet another contribution to the *Lessing-Mendelssohn-Gedenkbuch*, is interested in the question "Why is Nathan a Jew?" He notices how many writers have pondered this question before him and observes that it is important to know why the question would be of interest in the first place. He quotes a number of scholars on this matter: Kuno Fischer, Carl Schwarz, H.T. Rötscher, A.M. Goldschmidt, Julian Schmidt, David Friedrich Strauß, Karl Hase, Hermann Hettner, and Carl Hebler. Some wonder whether Nathan is the play's hero *because* he is Jewish, while others ask themselves whether he is the hero *despite* being a Jew? Bodek then goes back to Boccaccio and concludes that Lessing simply followed the story as suggested by his source. Melchisidek, the model for Nathan, was a Jew; so why should Lessing have changed it, Bodek reasons, unless he wanted to contradict his own philosophy of tolerance?

Two years after the celebrations in 1879, the one hundredth anniversary of Lessing's death was commemorated. Again, many a speech was given and article published on this subject. The Lessing scholar Klaus Bohnen has collected and compared texts from 1781, 1881, and 1981 (1982). For the most part, these texts are newspaper articles and lectures written on the occasion of Lessing's death and the centenary and bicentenary of it. What the writers all have in common, Bohnen finds, is that they use Lessing with equal conviction to further their differing causes (178). The year 1881 is different, however, inasmuch as the tension between Jews and German nationalists had escalated and so dominated much of the literary criticism of the day.

Ludwig Auerbach, who spoke on the hundredth anniversary of Lessing's death day (1881), cannot help but mention that hatred and envy have surfaced against the Jews. How should Jews deal with this? he asks. What advice might Nathan give, were he alive today? Maybe he would advise the Jews, Auerbach suggests, not to despair and to have faith in the humanity of their fellow Germans. Jews are not alone, he points out, because the "better" Germans are on their side; they are themselves ashamed of the "Judenfrage."

Not everyone felt as optimistic as Ludwig Auerbach. Berthold Auerbach, for example, expressed his hopelessness in a letter dated January 22, 1881. He dreads the thought of having to give yet another talk about Lessing in front of a Jewish audience, he writes (Bertold Auerbach 1881). One should not use Lessing to deny the reality of renewed and vehement Jew-baiting, he says.

b: Anti-Semitic Critics

At the same time that Jews and liberals hoped for or even believed themselves to have reached an understanding and a situation of mutual acceptance, the anti-Semites began to retaliate. Hans-Günter Zmarzlik's essay "Antisemitismus im Deutschen Kaiserreich [Anti-Semitism in the German Empire]" deals with what he considers the first serious anti-Semitic phase in Germany (1982, 255). In 1879 the "Antisemiten Liga [Anti-Semitic League]" was called into being. Ironically, this league originated in a Lessing club (cf. Zimmermann 1986, 185). How was it possible that Lessing's work could be used by anti-Semites to support their cause? Hector de Grounsilliers, one of the members, shed some light on the process. In a lecture to the club, he interpreted *Nathan the Wise* as a basically anti-Jewish play (Zimmermann 1986, 186). The very word *anti-Semitic* was popularized by the cofounder of the league, Wilhelm Marr.[2] In avoiding the word *Jewish* and replacing it with the racial term *Semites*, the focus was shifted away from the religious to the racial (Zimmermann 1986, 185). In his book *Sieg des Judenthums über das Germanentum* [Judaism's Victory over Germanness] ([7]1879), Marr makes this distinction clear. He graciously defends the Jews against religiously motivated animosities while declaring war to the "Verjudung" (Jewification) of German society (8). It would be difficult to find an equally opinionated, prejudiced, and demagogic book as this one. Marr, a political agitator and outspoken atheist, was married three times to women of Jewish descent. When he married a fourth time, this time a non-Jewish woman, he "broke forth with a barrage of racist antisemitism," as Paul Lawrence Rose writes in his *Revolutionary Antisemitism in Germany* (1990, 288). Marr repeatedly asserts his innocent intentions. He merely wants to state a cultural and historical fact, he claims (3). His dream might have been that future generations would recognize him as the prophet who predicted the Jewish victory long before its time. Or maybe he wanted to paint such a gloomy picture of how Jews were taking over the German state that his readers would feel compelled to intervene. In any event, to enrage his German readers further, Marr pretends to hold a stoic and resigned position: the victory of Jews over Germans is such a certainty that

---

[2] "The term 'anti-semitic' was actually coined by the Jewish writer M. Steinschneider ... in 1860" (Rose 1990, 288).

any attempt to prevent it would be futile (47f.). The book ends with a dramatic "Finis Germaniae [The End of Germany]" (48). In the course of his deliberations, Marr mentions Lessing. Like de Grounsilliers, he assumes an attitude of respect toward Lessing, yet he succeeds in reinterpreting every one of Lessing's positions. *Nathan the Wise*, in particular, is quoted as proof that Lessing recognized the Jewish question as a social problem (17). Even Lessing, Marr holds, made the connection between Jewishness and financial power when he invented Nathan as a "Geldnegozianten [money negotiator]." It would therefore be ludicrous, says Marr, to take *Nathan the Wise* as a stepping stone toward Jewish emancipation.

Another writer of the time, Richard Mayr, presented *Nathan the Wise* in a more negative light. In his *Beiträge zur Beurtheilung G.E. Lessing's* [Contributions on the Evaluation of G.E. Lessing] (1880), Mayr pretends to take an "enlightened" look at Lessing as well as at the Jewish question. He begins his study with an analysis of *Nathan the Wise*, focusing especially on the flaws and contradictions of the ring parable. For example, he asks how the father in the story, a senile weakling who cannot chose among his sons, could symbolize God (23)? The judge does not fare better in Mayr's eyes: his portrayal as a modest man is simply false, Mayr asserts. He thinks the judge is impertinent (26). First he declares all three rings to be copies (which is impossible according to the story, Mayr adds), and then he asks the sons to believe in them anyway (27f.). How could the rings have ever developed their magic power, since they were not given to the chosen son in the first place? Second, the sons are in a double bind. Either they take their respective brothers to be pitiful fools believing in false rings or they must harbor doubts about their own rings — which would again end in the impossibility of releasing the ring's powers (29). In a word, Mayr declares Lessing's story a failure. One cannot believe in the equality of all religions and at the same time insist that individual believers should remain faithful to their own religion. Therefore, Mayr concludes, Lessing was not really an Enlightenment author but a reactionary (34). In the latter part of the book it becomes clear that Mayr himself favors atheism (127f.). Likewise, other statements make Mayr appear quite modern — at first glance. He argues against antiatheist laws (129f.), for example, as well as against nationalism and intolerance (136f.). He also distances himself from anti-Semitism, an "absurd and evil movement" (138). But Mayr believes at the same time that a society must defend itself against foreign and heterogeneous elements. The Jewish question, which has existed for up to three thousand years (as Mayr finds it necessary to point out), is thus not a political question (why not?) but a social one (139ff.). It is the Jews' own fault that they attract such anger and hatred (142, 145). Why don't they assimilate, why do they refuse progress, why, to give a practical example, do they refuse to use soap? Mayr asks (141). Statements such as these reveal Mayr as an anti-Semite and his earlier thesis — tolerance needs to be replaced by justice and reason (120) — turns out to be hypocritical. Mayr's evaluation of the Jews is contradictory at best. He blames them for having followed Nathan's advice to hold on to their ancient beliefs (36, 144), and at the same time he criticizes their desire for acceptance into society and into the higher professions (143). These comments were made at a time when, in reality, Jews were afraid that they might lose the opportunity to enter higher positions such as university posts (cf. Boehlich 1965, 249). Mayr's suggested solution for the "Jewish problem" is the following: "Erst wenn alle aufgehört haben werden, Juden zu sein, wird die Judenfrage definitiv gelöst sein [Only when all Jews will have stopped being Jews will the Jewish question be solved]" (145). To give him the benefit of the doubt, let us assume that he means assimilation rather than holocaust.

A similar technique to the one used by Ludwig Auerbach — putting words into the mouth of a literary figure — is employed by Julian Schmidt, a well-known liberal critic of his time. Schmidt's contribution to the Lessing celebrations in 1881 reveals, however, that he is a representative of the faction opposed to Auerbach's. He writes that the question he would have liked to present Lessing with is whether Jews might not actually be responsible for the prejudice that exists against them (Schmidt 1881, 73). Like Richard Mayr, Schmidt would like to blame the victim, even though he also admits that no person has chosen his or her fate: "Der Einzelne freilich hat sein Schicksal nicht gemacht, nicht nach seiner Wahl ist er Jude geworden, aber zu tragen hat er das Schicksal als ob er es selber gewählt hätte [Of course, the individual did not create his own fate, he did not become a Jew by choice, but he has to bear this fate as if he had chosen it himself]" (76). Of course, Schmidt has an idea of how Lessing would react. He would be receptive to any new hypothesis, Schmidt says, even if it challenged one of Lessing's own ideas (73f.). This is a rather absurd statement. Lessing said that destruction is part of the creative process, as Schmidt reminds his readers, but that does not prove that Lessing would have condoned prejudice. No, this is Schmidt's argument, one that he shared with a large part of the German population at the time. Granted, he concedes, a Jew has not chosen his or her fate. But the Jews are guilty anyway, because they spent a thousand years in isolation, fancying themselves a chosen people (75). Once more, Schmidt calls on Lessing to be his witness, referring to *Nathan the Wise* in particular. The twist in Schmidt's interpretation is indeed surprising. Nathan was invented by Lessing as an ideal yet real character, Schmidt suggests, in order to shame Moses Mendelssohn, who embodied superstition and arrogance toward Christianity (78). Schmidt thus implies that *Nathan the Wise* was written as an attack on Jewish superstition and arrogance.

The most radical anti-Semitic critic of Lessing was Eugen Dühring, whose anti-Semitism surpasses that of all the other writers so far mentioned. He seems to have enjoyed widespread popularity: a talk of his in 1880 was accompanied, as he boastingly recalls, by unusually strong applause. This talk was later transformed into a book, *Die Überschätzung Lessing's und seiner Befassung mit Literatur* [The Overvaluation of Lessing and his literary criticism] (^{2}1906). Dühring's opinion of Lessing is negative. He accepts him neither as a poet nor a critic, let alone as a genius (3, 19). Were it not for the "Judenreclame [the Jewish press]," he writes, Lessing would not have been successful at all because most Germans are left cold by him (67). Dühring takes this idea further by sharing the "general knowledge" that Jews praise not what is good but what serves them — even if it is the very worst (69). And this is just what Lessing was: the very worst. *Minna von Barnhelm*, an "alleged" comedy, is a miserable play in every respect (21). *Emilia Galotti* enjoys the questionable praise of being the "least bad" (4). The works that displeased Dühring the most are *Die Juden*, *Nathan the Wise*, and *Die Erziehung des Menschengeschlechts*. Dühring accuses Lessing of falsely flattering the Jews while at the same time depicting Germans as stupid. According to him, *Nathan the Wise* would be better entitled "Melchisedek der Verschmitzte [Melchisedek the Rogue]." For once, Lessing has depicted a Jewish character according to nature: Nathan is rich, greedy, and cunning (77). Dühring argues that in the ring parable, Judaism is raised over the other two religions (77). After all these accusations, one will not be surprised to hear that Dühring also thought badly of Lessing as a person, imputing that Lessing was of mixed blood, possibly a tenth part Jewish (93).

After all this serious criticism of Lessing, and after Dühring's stupid and skittish text in particular, it is refreshing to come across a satire. By way of persiflage, Fritz Mauthner hopes to show how ridiculous Dühring's malicious attack on Lessing really is (1886). Mauthner imitates Dühring's approach by portraying Goethe as a pitiful and unoriginal writer, a scoundrel. He was probably born in the Frankfurt ghetto to Jewish parents, he writes. And Schiller? One look at his long nose suffices to raise suspicion. But in the end, Mauthner does not feel comfortable enough to leave the satire as is. Dühring's text, after all, sounds just as unreasonable. To avoid any doubt about his own position, Mauthner concludes his text with an angry invective against Dühring and Mayr. Mauthner may have been emotionally excited, as Barner *et al.* say (^{5}1987, 414). Why should he not have been? His intuition is almost prophetic, after all, when he suspects his opponents of secretly plotting the murder of all Jews some December night.

It is noteworthy that Dühring's interpretation did not supply a model for later literary criticism. A good example of how Lessing's reputation improved with anti-Semites is Adolf Bartels, who later became an outspoken National-Socialist and enjoyed high respect as a writer and critic. The anti-Semitic sentiments expressed in his book *Lessing und die Juden* [Lessing and the Jews] (1918) are the equal of Dühring's. Yet Lessing fares much better in this book. Bartels reinstates him as a poet of significance and contradicts the thesis that Lessing was partly Jewish (25). *Nathan the Wise* must, of course, be repudiated as too pro-Jewish, but even so Bartels recognizes some good in the drama. He fancies himself conciliatory by favoring Erich Schmidt's interpretation over Dühring's. If Lessing was friends with Jews, it was not his fault, Bartels concedes. After all, he was young, impressionable, lonesome — defenseless in the hands of the Jews (69). From here, it is only one small step to the assertion that Lessing would certainly be an anti-Semite in Bartels's own time (343).[3]

[3] A revised version of *Lessing und die Juden* appeared in 1934. In it, Bartels admits that his objections to Lessing have since increased (228). Yet he is still convinced that Lessing would have become an enemy of Jews in Bartels's days (237). If there is indeed the need for a "new Lessing" (Goethe's words), Bartels would like to be this man himself (237).

5: From Empire to Republic

a: Franz Mehring

BETWEEN 1871 AND 1933 most literary critics concerned themselves with abstract, aesthetically-oriented interpretations. One exception was Franz Mehring, a materialist thinker, who was a particularly important Lessing scholar. His *Lessing-Legende* first appeared in 1893 and went into several editions in the first decade of the new century. But it is not only through its publication dates that this book connects the centuries. Mehring, the nineteenth-century writer, is hoping for a brighter political future while he concerns himself with the life, work, and time of Lessing. Most important, however, Mehring is interested in uncovering the "legend" that his contemporaries created by placing Lessing on a pedestal next to the Prussian king Frederick the Great. As we have seen, writers such as Heinrich von Treitschke and Adolf Stahr referred to Lessing and Frederick as their heroes. Mehring, however, has only contempt for these writers and for the bourgeoisie of the nineteenth century they represented. Lacking any backbone, he sneers, this class failed their revolution and their liberation. Instead, they traded self-esteem for nationalism, placing themselves under the Prussian flag and revering Frederick the Great as the hero who led Prussia to glory (306). Mehring refuses to give Frederick this kind of recognition. Analyzing political, social, and economic data from Frederick's era, he arrives at the conclusion that none of it makes Frederick appear an enlightened, just, and tolerant sovereign. If there was an enlightened king, Mehring continues, it was Frederick's father, Wilhelm II. Wilhelm at least made honest attempts at integrating the bourgeois class into his administration (115). Frederick hated the middle classes and reinstated the "Junkers," Prussian squires, in their privileges (69, 79). Mehring also criticizes the notion that Frederick granted freedom of the press and of religion for humanitarian reasons. He convincingly argues that Frederick was motivated by pragmatism (71ff.). The decree for religious freedom, for example, was not intended to liberate anybody but to expand Frederick's army. Likewise, the press was allowed to criticize every *other* monarch but not Frederick himself. Mehring concludes poignantly that Frederick contradicted and violated every Enlightenment principle. Yet the nineteenth century loved to think of Frederick and Lessing as allies. Lessing was, if anything, Frederick's absolute counterpart, not a Prussian nor a patriot (78), Mehring writes. He traces the myth of their alliance to writers such as Goethe, Gervinus, Lassalle, Danzel, and Stahr.

None of these critics, however, angers him as much as do Scherer and, even more, Erich Schmidt. In fact, Mehring's book developed out of several articles he had written to review Schmidt's biography *Lessing* (1884-1886). Schmidt's servile attitude and impudence infuriate Mehring. Lessing would never, Mehring exclaims, have ingratiated himself with his king or with Voltaire in the way Schmidt describes (239).

Mehring then adds his own interpretation of Lessing to break with the "legend" once and for all. His book does offer valuable new insights. Never before was Lessing's position so clearly put into its historical framework. The economic and political information Mehring offers helps explain many of Lessing's invectives against patriotism, the Prussian state, and racial intolerance. Lessing's self-assurance is linked to the beginning of bourgeois class-consciousness (218). Mehring's analysis also makes plausible what Lessing's motivation might have been for participating in the war and why he used soldiers as heroes in so many of his dramas. The military, Mehring explains, was the only class that was allowed any individuality and independence under Frederick. Soldiers thus realized some of the dreams that motivated the bourgeois class (265).

As well devised and convincing as most of Mehring's arguments are, his book also dwells on some points whose validity is dubious. He takes his appropriation of Lessing as a political and materialist author too far when he calls Lessing a proletarian (239), for example, or when he compares him with Karl Marx (78, 259). Also, one would hope that Mehring would not only break with the ideological position of his adversaries but that he would also depart from some of the clichés they used. Unfortunately, he holds on to such notions as Lessing's "manliness" and his heroic steadfastness in the face of his tragic fate. Other flaws are even more serious. Mehring not only blames the German bourgeoisie but also accuses "philo-Semitism" for the creation of a Lessing legend. His attacks on the "philo-Semites" are a little hard to digest, and even his East German editors admit with some embarrassment that these passages might strike the modern reader as peculiar. What is especially objectionable is Mehring's thesis that in its denial of class difference, philo-Semitism is just as dangerous as anti-Semitism. When he talks about Mendelssohn, Mehring even sounds anti-Semitic himself. His fiery enthusiasm for the free-born Lessing strikingly contrasts with his unsympathetic description of the Jewish-born Mendelssohn, who is still "dragging his broken chains" (260). His scorn for Moses's pride at having moved up from Jewish haggler to German philistine (275) puts his Marxist and class-conscious sincerity in question.

Mehring's analysis also falls short when it comes to interpreting the texts. Some of the observations made are provoking, interesting, and accurate:

Mehring interprets *Philotas* and *Minna von Barnhelm* as outright attacks on and satires of Frederick's military state (271, 283). He also for the first time points to the social relevance of some of Lessing's theoretical writing. In general, however, Mehring really talks about Lessing the character, not the writer. There seems to be a measure of agreement between his and Friedrich Schlegel's positions. It was Schlegel who had said the famous words: "Er selbst war mehr wert, als alle seine Talente" (see above, p. 17), and this seems to be exactly where Mehring stands, too. Whenever he refers to Lessing's writing, he becomes apologetic and evasive. He declares Lessing's aesthetics and his philosophy outdated (30), making him a scholar instead of a poet (218). Thus, Lessing's dramatic writing is not even accepted as literature. To say that Lessing was politically motivated is one thing, but to assume, as Mehring does, that preaching and teaching were his only motivations, that he used the stage for this sole purpose (220), simply makes no sense.

Mehring does not have a high opinion of *Nathan the Wise*. Since he only sees the political motivation behind the play, Mehring cannot appreciate the "holprige Verse [stumbling verse]" (344) and says he would have preferred prose. In a 1909 essay Mehring comes back to *Nathan the Wise* once more. The years between the texts did not improve Mehring's opinion of the drama. Now even the plot is criticized as too romantic, too improbable (421). Neither has Mehring's bad opinion of Moses Mendelssohn changed. He rejects the idea that Nathan is intended as a portrayal of Mendelssohn (419). Instead, Mehring searches for Lessing's own personality traits in the male characters. Thus, Mehring's literary analysis turns out to be, once again, a characterization, even an idealization, of Lessing. Mehring sees Lessing's dialectical thinking exemplified by Nathan's preference for dialogue. Likewise, Lessing's temper and goodness are found in Saladin, his freedom and pride in the Templar, his nobility and savagery in the dervish Al-Hafi, and his humility in the Lay Brother (422).

As previously mentioned, one of the critics fiercely attacked by Mehring was Erich Schmidt. His biography of Lessing first appeared in 1884 and 1886 and was revised for a second edition in 1899. Karl Guthke calls it *the* authoritative work on Lessing but at the same time admits that there is nothing really original about it (Guthke [3]1979, 82). Schmidt aims for a moderate viewpoint and turns away in disgust from the theological and racial disputes Lessing's work has unfairly been made the center of by both left- and right-wing critics who "violate" the integrity of his work to prove their extreme ideas (1899, 398). The illusion of being able to escape political realities or any ideological position whatsoever, for that matter, is typical for Schmidt as well as for his contemporaries. That is not to say that literary criticism is any more objective than it was before. "Post-Mehring" critics are just as nationalistic, to give one example, as were the writers attacked in *Die Lessing-Legende*. In other words, Lessing is still revered as the great Prussian hero.

b: The First World War

Toward the beginning of the twentieth century Germany indulged itself in militaristic dreams of power. This emerging ideology aligned itself with pro-Prussian sentiments and was quickly appropriated by some Lessing critics. Friedrich Lienhard means it as the highest praise when he says in 1907 that Lessing embodies "gutes Preußentum [good Prussian values]." While he takes Lessing seriously neither as a poet nor as a philosopher, Lienhard does call him by the militaristic title "Kamerad" (419). Even Lessing's relationship with his wife, Eva König, is best described as "comradeship," Lienhard informs us. He takes further liberties in reinterpreting Lessing's sentiments when he declares Lessing's years in military service the most genuine and fulfilling period of his life. Theodor Kappstein takes this militaristic infatuation farther and surprises today's readers with a number of martial metaphors. His talk, tellingly titled "Der kriegerische Lessing [The belligerent Lessing]" (1915), uses similes such as *signal, torchbearer, beacon, wrestler,* and *sword carrier.* Lessing is even compared to war itself: "Lessing ist ein Freiheitskrieg, ein Befreiungssieg [Lessing is a war of liberty, a victory of liberation]" (440). Likewise, *Nathan the Wise* is interpreted as an act of war. Kappstein reasons that it is with this last drama that Lessing the "army chaplain" finally, after a life full of fighting, wanted to preach peace.

After the First World War, after four years of death and destruction in Europe, intellectuals sounded less militaristic, at least for the moment. Neither is there any echo of the economic and social chaos that prevailed in Weimar Germany in Gottfried Fittbogen's essay entitled "Die Religion Lessings [Lessings Religion]" (1923). Fittbogen bases his interpretation of *Nathan the Wise* on the ring parable, the "Keimzelle [germ cell]" of the play (64). In it he finds a new, humane religion of love, gentleness, peaceableness, and harmony (72). But as gentle as he sounds, Fittbogen barely hides his antipathy for Nathan. He finds Nathan's emphasis on his own virtues obtrusive (84), he is put off when Nathan is moved to tears by his own good deed (86), and he wishes that Nathan would admit the mistakes he made in raising Recha (90). Recha, on the other hand, represents the new theory more purely. She has made the step beyond positive religion that her father has not been able to take (73f.). This difference may exist, Fittbogen hypothesizes, because Nathan expresses some of Lessing's personal struggle. After hardship and loss (Lessing lost his newborn son and then his wife in 1777-1778; Nathan lost his wife and children in a murderous attack by Christians), both were able to accept the will of God (90f.). Their path to the new religion leads through tragedy, one might conclude Fittbogen's thesis, while Recha embraces humanism out of the pureness of her heart.

Another Weimar critic who longed for a world of Classicist calm and self-control was Fritz Brüggemann. In his contribution to the *Zeitschrift für Deutschkunde* (1925), Brüggemann argues that wisdom, not tolerance, constitutes the play's main idea (74). One must grant Brüggemann that Lessing named Nathan a "wise," not a tolerant man in the title. Brüggemann examines Nathan's wisdom and finds that it is captured in his mastery over his life — he is neither controlled by external factors nor by his own emotions. Thus, Nathan symbolizes the golden mean between sentimentality and passion, on the one hand, and escapism on the other (78ff.). This harmonious ideal is reminiscent of Classicism, but it does not allow for the consideration of religious tolerance and cosmopolitanism. Brüggemann accepts these ideas only as the by-products and after-effects of Nathan's wisdom (82).

c: Before Hitler's Seizure of Power

Lessing's two hundredth birthday was celebrated in 1929 with lectures and essays. As Germany became more and more isolated from the rest of the world, Lessing came to symbolize a brave Germany surrounded by enemies. Some liberals took the chance to shyly[1] remind their listeners and readers one last time of the values of Humanism before National Socialism swept all those thoughts away. Intellectuals such as Theodor Heuss, Thomas Mann, and Hugo von Hofmannsthal raised their voice of rationality and specifically referred to *Nathan the Wise*.[2] At the same time, they used some of the same attributes and

---

[1] So shyly that Werner Rieck wonders whether their meek tone did not help eliminate contradictions inherent in Lessing as well as in the social and political order of the time (1984, 350f.).

[2] Other participants in the celebrations in 1929 were Ernst Elster, Friedrich Gundolf, Julius Petersen, Theodorus Cornelis van Stockum, Walter von Molo, Ricarda Huch, and Julius Bab. Most of these only touch on *Nathan the Wise* in

clichés that the National Socialists were employing: both sides kept up the image of Lessing as a manly fighter. Theodor Heuss's essay is typical of the helpless and detached stance of the liberals of his era. He feels uncomfortable with the way Lessing is being utilized for the patriotic and political purposes of the right (Heuss 1929, 447), yet he also disagrees with Franz Mehring, who criticized just that Prussian myth. Mehring, an outspoken Marxist, appears too polemical to Heuss (446). What remains is a call for "das Bürgerliche als Gesinnung [bourgeois values]" (447). Heuss suggests that we rid ourselves of our diffuse and opaque conception of bourgeois values, but he then only offers adjectives that are diffuse and opaque: Lessing's humanity is "young, fresh, courageous and self-confident" (447). This humanity is above all noted in *Nathan the Wise*. Heuss must have thought that a loving understanding of the "foreign" other (447) would be able to cut through in those unloving times.

In one of the two Lessing essays Thomas Mann published in 1929, he gives the enemy a name. The spirit of Lessing, Mann claims, can help overcome fascism (1929b, 141). What makes Lessing so timely is his dialectics rather than his abstract humanism as expressed in *Nathan the Wise*, Mann says. But what really interests him in Lessing is the justification of Mann's own position. The dispute over whether Lessing was a poet or not seems to him an annoying "querelle allemande" (1929a, 449). The answer is easy. Lessing is a "Schriftsteller" (1929a, 450), just as Mann is himself. The modern term *Schriftsteller* (writer) replaces the term *Dichter* (poet) favored by conservative literary scholars. That Lessing embodies the prototype of the modern intellectual makes him, in Mann's eyes, a forerunner of modernity (1929a, 448f.).

When Mann declares Lessing to be the prototype of the European intellectual, he quickly passes over the question of how good a German Lessing really was. He has only scorn for the pedantic attempts of German critics to pin down *their* Lessing (the "querelle allemande"). Hugo von Hofmannsthal shares Mann's indignation at the public's reaction to Lessing but thinks that the very tension between Lessing and the German nation is Lessing's significance.[3] Unfortunately, this statement is not further elaborated. He could have made an important point about the challenge Lessing embodied for his readers and critics. Horst Steinmetz, in his anthology *Lessing — ein unpoetischer Dichter* [Lessing — An Unpoetic Poet] (1969) expresses

passing, however. (Cf. Rieck 1984, 350-360; Richter 1930; Otto Mann 1935.)

[3] "Seine Bedeutung für die Nation liegt in seinem Widerspruch zu ihr" (1929, 454).

something similar when he says that it is the reactions he provoked, not Lessing himself, that are typically German (42). Two hundred years of Lessing interpretation are representative of Germany's values and basic ideologies. Hofmannsthal died the same year he wrote his Lessing essay and so did not live to see fascism develop. One wonders what his role would have been if he had lived. He, too, shows a preference for the "herb Männliche, leuchtend Metallische [harshly masculine, brilliantly metallic]" so many people have praised in Lessing (452). Both Mann and Hofmannsthal get from Lessing a confirmation of their own views on literature. Mann discovers the "Schriftsteller" in Lessing, and Hofmannsthal, the author of such well-known comedies as *Der Rosenkavalier* and *Der Schwierige*, realizes that no one has yet understood *Nathan the Wise* in the way it was intended: as the most ingenious comedy German literature possesses (453). Hofmannsthal here has the same thought as Friedrich Schiller, who also detected the comic element in *Nathan the Wise* (see above, p. 24), but Hofmannsthal reacts more positively than Schiller, the author of classical tragedies.

The twentieth century also brought forth another wave of attempts to understand Lessing and *Nathan the Wise* from a theological perspective. Ernst Cassirer (1929) finds in *Nathan the Wise* the answer to a theological problem: he asks whether religious belief is based on eternal truth, coincidence, or reason (97f.). Lessing's answer to this question is different from both the orthodox position and Mendelssohn's position, Cassirer claims. While the orthodox theory simply declares the church and the bible to be ultimately and eternally valid (100), Mendelssohn accepts that some things cannot be revealed to humankind (103). Lessing's position, on the other hand, is that there is no ultimate proof of religion's truth; instead, truth must be re-created dialectically as time goes on (107). In this light, Cassirer understands the judge's decision in *Nathan the Wise* as a humble respect for religion rooted in the knowledge that proof will come, but in the future and only to those who deserve it (111). Such a theological interpretation of the play goes hand in hand with Cassirer's emphasis on Lessing's importance for theological history: he declares Lessing the creator of a new kind of Protestantism (113). Protestantism, he explains, has progressed by defending against and reacting to Lessing's provocative ideas about the individual's responsibility in history.

Hans Leisegang's interpretation also centers on religious questions and even touches on mysticism. He refers once more to Nathan's acceptance of his fate. After losing his family to the Christian murderers, Nathan finds what he believes to be a Christian baby and adopts her (1931, 118). It was this "good deed" that Fittbogen had criticized. Against Fittbogen, Leisegang holds that at this point Lessing touches the principles of mysticism. Lessing, Leisegang writes, rediscovered the mystic root of Christianity, the "Liebesevangelium [Gospel of Love]" (123). *Nathan the Wise* thus teaches love (124), and Nathan is the instrument of Providence sent to teach reason (126). "Das Ganze ist eine Theodizee [The whole thing is a theodicy]" (126). But Leisegang does not end, as did Cassirer, by declaring Lessing a new type of Protestant. Lessing's message, Leisegang says, is the proclamation of the "fourth" religion (130). Consequently, the parable does not really fit Lessing's purpose (131). What Lessing should have done, he says, is incorporate a fourth ring into the story (131). One might argue that the alternative to the three religions suggested by the parable may not be another religion but something different, which would not have to be symbolized by a ring.

Benno von Wiese, renowned for many seminal works written in the interwar period, published several texts on Lessing. As did Leisegang before him, Wiese searches for Lessing's worldview in *Nathan the Wise*. He differentiates, however, between the philosophical perspective expressed in the play and its theological implications, the latter being only of secondary concern (Wiese 1931, 133). Wiese's concentration on the parable as the key to the understanding of the play makes him neglect the action, which he sees as only an illustration of the play's message (134). Nevertheless, it is the characters of the play that Wiese interprets, not the parable. He evaluates the characters on a scale according to their degree of humanity, to their readiness for friendship. Nathan, as the incarnation of humanism, takes the top position. He is capable of friendship, which means he is capable of recognizing the human being in another person (137f.). Doing so may appear to be easy, writes Wiese, and it is, yet it is at the same time difficult because one needs much strength to overcome prejudice (138). Once achieved, this position is as much resignation (giving up the hopes and dreams of a different path of life) as it is acceptance of God's will (141). The humanist philosophy outlined in *Nathan the Wise* corresponds to the humanism of the eighteenth century, he goes on to say. This humanism is characterized by the rejection of the idea that individuals are bound to one religion from birth, by the emphasis on intellect, and by optimism. These three characteristics, von Wiese continues, correspond to the worldview of the Enlightenment: a belief in a truth which surpasses history, in the autonomy of reason, and in a harmonious world (145ff.). Finally, the world is seen as predetermined and an aim is recognized which may be called, Wiese suggests, morality. In accordance with the ideology of the Enlightenment, Lessing arrived at a belief in natural religion and in a humanism that can help people to submit to Providence, Wiese writes.[4]

---

[4] In another essay, published in 1932, Wiese picks up this thought once more: "Humanität ist also die sittliche Selbstentfaltung der Person auf Grund ihrer freien Einwilligung in die vernünftigen Gesetze des Ganzen (in den Willen Gottes)" (174).

6: 1933-1945

a: National Socialist Criticism

WHEN THE NATIONAL SOCIALISTS seized power in 1933, one of their immediate goals was the "Gleichschaltung" of all aspects of public life. As far as the cultural sector was concerned, this goal meant taking control not only of newspapers, radio stations, theater, and cinemas but also of schools and other institutions of higher learning — a task more or less completed by 1935 (cf. Zimmermann 1985, 280). On the university level faculty, courses, and reading materials were "sorted out" according to racial and ideological criteria. Among the disciplines, German studies, called "Deutschwissenschaft," became especially important (cf. Conrady 1967) since the decisions made here were perceived to have far-reaching repercussions in other areas of public life. Students would not only learn how to interpret Germany's cultural history in light of National Socialist ideology, they would, in turn, become teachers themselves and educate future generations. Proof that "Gleichschaltung" was mostly successful is the fact that censorship came not only from above but often from the students and faculty themselves: they would object to a professor or to reading materials for racial or political reasons. German departments readily adhered to the new criteria and used or even created nationalistic and racial terminologies that could be used by others in political arguments. *Gemeinschaft*, for example, was the term of choice for community, as was *volkseigen* for societal and *Dichter* for writer or poet. Considering that German Studies developed in the nineteenth century and began embracing nationalist, idealist, and conservative ideologies right from the start, one might even speak of a predisposition of the discipline for National Socialism (cf. Ziegler 1965, 156; Lämmert 1967, 21; Vondung 1973, 105; Lecke 1980, 195).

Even though one cannot really talk about *the* literary theory of National Socialism, some general interpretative techniques can be identified. "Völkische Literaturkritik" used concepts that were developed in the early twentieth century. The antibourgeois attitude of National Socialism dated back to earlier decades, and so did the nationalism that prevailed in literary studies (Berman 1985, 257). Even the obsession with race was well established before

1933. Josef Nadler's famous literary history, first published in 1913, is a case in point.

Nadler is occupied with identifying authors' racial backgrounds. He considers the value of any given author properly expressed only if his or her origin is taken into account. Heinz Otto Burger takes this notion further in 1934 by demanding that literary studies foster the racial self-identity of the "Gemeinschaft," the community (462). Once literature was thus racially classified, non-Aryan writers could be ejected from literary history. Other authors were rejected for their political opinions. But even after this first period of "sorting out," a wealth of German literature remained that embraced ideals quite different from nationalist or National Socialist ones. Since it could not all be rejected, it had to be reinterpreted. This was what happened to Lessing. The image of Lessing during the years 1933 to 1945 is quite exemplary of the method used by literary critics at the time.

Interpretation of Lessing during the Third Reich was not dramatically new. In many respects, it referred directly back to nineteenth-century traditions. On the other hand, the emphasis on race brought with it a new twist (cf. Grimm 1975, 170; Barner *et al.* [5]1987, 416). Before Lessing could be heralded as a German writer and a Nordic hero, his life and work had to be distorted. Certain aspects of Lessing's thinking, his humanism and tolerant attitude especially, could not possibly please the new ruling powers. His friendship with the Jewish Moses Mendelssohn caused some considerable headache. Theodor Fritsch, whose *Handbuch der Judenfrage* [Handbook on the Jewish question] went through forty-nine (!) editions between 1887 and 1944, regrets that Lessing and *Nathan the Wise* supplied Jews with an argument *for* emancipation and enlightenment (Fritsch [38]1935, 84).

How did National Socialist critics manage to erase Lessing's friendship with Moses Mendelssohn? A text by Hellmuth Fechner (1935) is illustrative. Fechner holds that Lessing was not a liberal, was neither an "Aufklärer [enlightener]" nor a friend of Jews, a "Judenfreund." What was he? "Fallible," is Fechner's answer. Whatever Lessing said in support of enlightened ideas about racial tolerance can be disqualified as an error. He might have made a few such errors, but who would want to list them all? Fechner is generous and open to forgive. This approach was employed by others. Again and again, critics excuse Lessing's sympathy for the Jews as a small mistake due either to misjudgment or to a lack of proper understanding of the Jewish race. Mathilde Ludendorff goes even a step further in her popular biography of Lessing (1937). She defends Lessing's support of the Jews as an expression of his good character. Lessing could simply not, she writes, comprehend the depth of Jewish meanness and hypocrisy (1937, 18).

She regrets that *Nathan the Wise* was directed against the Christian orthodox rather than against the Jews, who were the real "wire-pullers" for intolerance and conceit (164). Not only was Lessing's naivety taken advantage of by his Jewish contemporaries, but later generations of Jews also misinterpreted and falsified his work for their own purposes (38, 58, 70, 164). Finally, Ludendorff asserts that the Jews and/or the Freemasons killed not only Lessing's wife Eva König but also Lessing himself (118, 125, 210).

Walther Linden, in a literary history of the same year, also regrets the error Lessing made when supporting Jews and Freemasons (266). He quickly adds that this error should not undercut the importance of his achievement for the German people (266). Linden argues that Lessing was misled when he thought of Jews in religious terms: they are actually a race apart (265). His admiration for Lessing's "German" merits is shared by Hellmuth Langenbucher (1937). Langenbucher, however, is less forgiving than Linden and hesitates to excuse all of Lessing's views. Instead, he emphasizes that Lessing deserves both approval and criticism (77).

Ernst Suter (1938) forgives Lessing because ambition necessarily entails following some false trails at first: "Lessing hat viel geirrt, weil er viel gestrebt hat [Lessing erred a lot because he strived a lot]" (416). He tries to appease his contemporaries by arguing that historical figures could not possibly be expected to have reached today's level of ideological maturity. If the National Socialist standard was applied to every person in the past and if no errors were forgiven, who would be left (416)? At the same time, Suter brings in another argument. Maybe, he writes, Lessing was not such a friend of the Jews after all. If Lessing had really been interested in mixing the two races, he would have written a different ending to his early play *The Jews:* When the honest businessman unmasks some criminal scoundrels who had disguised themselves as Jews and reveals that he himself is a Jew, the baron would not have withheld the hand of his daughter (415). Suter forgets to take into consideration that a marriage between a German and a Jew was forbidden by law when Lessing was writing his play. Yet this is the same argument that Elisabeth Frenzel uses in her 1940 dissertation *Judengestalten auf der deutschen Bühne* [Jewish characters on the German stage]. Lessing was confused, Frenzel says, when he created a Jewish character and supplied him with German characteristics (58). Obviously, Frenzel does not consider it possible for a Jew to be German as well.

Werner Zimmermann's essay "Die Gestalt der Juden [The Jewish character]" (1940) employs once more all the techniques of the National Socialist whitewash. He asks his readers to consider that Lessing lived in a time when the great "disaster" began to take its course, in other words, the period when Jews began to infiltrate the German nation (253). Lessing, though an upright Prussian citizen, unwillingly helped create a Jew-friendly atmosphere that made the infiltration possible. Lessing only defended the Jewish race out of a natural inclination to take sides with the oppressed (250). Maybe, Zimmermann speculates, Lessing was influenced by the Jews around him who promoted the philosophy of Enlightenment. While Mendelssohn and other Jewish philosophers were hypocritical for wishing only to further the cause of the Jews to the exclusion of other races, Lessing overlooked their true motivation out of his deep fascination with the idea of tolerance (246). Zimmermann believes that Lessing's interest in the Jewish people was not as deep as commonly believed, that Lessing in fact had reservations about the poor and common Jews. To substantiate this allegation, Zimmermann raises the rhetorical question: Why did Lessing not use a *poor* Jew as protagonist in *Nathan the Wise* (252)? From here, Zimmermann takes a quick step and arrives at the following conclusion: 150 years later, Lessing would have been an anti-Semite (250).

Once Lessing had been "rescued," and his egalitarianism excused, critics of the National Socialist era could concentrate on what they saw as his more positive traits. What impressed them most was Lessing's alleged "nordic" character. The term *nordic* may sound vague and hollow to modern ears, but in the 1930s it was very precise. Burger labels Lessing thus because of his objective passion, his conscience, and his sense of humor (1934, 473). Likewise, Suter admires Lessing's willpower, his sober clarity, and his instinct to fight (1938). *Nordic* described manliness: Suter sums up his characterization of Lessing by saying that Lessing embodied the opposite of feminine enthusiasm (416). Similarly, Walther Linden calls Lessing one of the most masculine and rebellious spirits of German literature (1937, 256). As always when Lessing is idealized, it is especially his lonely, "heroic," and tragic life that touches the critics.

Moving beyond Lessing's personal characteristics, National Socialist writers and scholars found more points to substantiate their admiration in certain aspects of his work. Lessing's dedication to and struggle for a German theater is interpreted as a patriotic fight against the French. Paul Adams, for example, singles out Lessing's support of the "Germanic" Shakespeare — while National Socialists condemned "Welsh" cultures such as the French and Italian, they respected the English — and presents it as proof of his national "dependability" (1933, 152f.; cf. also Suter 1938, 418). Lessing's language and style of writing are also cited to corroborate the thesis that he was a truly German and nordic poet (cf. Grimm 1975, 171).

Above all, Lessing's plays were heralded in Hitler's Germany for Lessing's alleged nationalism. *Philotas* and *Minna von Barnhelm* especially impressed critics as patriotic dramas. Philotas and Tellheim were seen as heroes who represent Prussian, i.e., German honor (cf. Eckardt 1991, 72f.). Other plays, however, provoked less enthusiasm. *Emilia Galotti* stirred feelings of discomfort (cf. Frank 1973, 887). It could not be interpreted as patriotic, nor did the story quite fit the idea of Prussian honor. Even more, *The Jews* and *Nathan the Wise* irritated the scholars with their Jewish protagonists. Throughout the nineteenth century *Nathan the Wise* had been performed on stages and taught in schools. By 1890 there were several editions of the play specifically for schools (cf. König 1974, 135). In the late nineteenth and through the early twentieth century, however, pressure against the play mounted. A film version was heckled by a fascist mob in 1923 (cf. Loiperdinger 1982). In 1933 *Nathan the Wise* was banned from school curricula (cf. König 1974, 113; G. Grimm 1974, 35). Wilhelm Poethen made it clear in 1936 that neither *Emilia Galotti* nor *Nathan the Wise* belonged into the classroom. Instead, he suggested that students learn about patriotism and German style by the study of Lessing's better plays, fables, and theoretical writings such as *Hamburgische Dramaturgie* (24f.). Most textbook authors followed this suggestion and, in spite of the ban on *Nathan the Wise*, German school children in fact read more of Lessing than of many other famous authors (cf. Lauf-Immesberger 1987, 73).

To be fair one should mention that some critics dared to present a more balanced view of Lessing. Gerhard Fricke held a position of significant power as coeditor of the *Zeitschrift für Deutschkunde* [Journal for German Studies]. Even though he frequently made considerable concessions to the ideology in power, he avoided blunt generalizations and quick judgments. In a 1934 essay he argues against the National Socialist reinterpretation of history. Men ("Männer," not "Menschen") and events need to be seen without distortions for what they really were (371). Having said this, Fricke turns to *Nathan the Wise*, the work so obviously shunned by his contemporaries. He calls it Lessing's most personal and most telling work, his legacy (371). Lessing's legacy, Fricke explains, is his understanding of humanity, reason, and morality (373).

When it comes to Lessing's position against intolerance and fanaticism, Fricke begins to waver. At first his discussion of the issue sounds relatively objective, and he acknowledges the validity of Lessing's attacks on religious and historical concepts (375f.). He is disturbed, however, that Lessing seems to consider the national and religious origin of people as a "coincidence." Where Lessing sees free individuals, Fricke fears disintegration, lack of connectedness, and the isolation of the individual (378). In *Nathan the Wise*, for example, Fricke misses a "real" place, a place named or defined by nature, landscape, or history (380). Even the characters, Fricke complains, are ideal and unnatural (381). Because Fricke insists on the characters' racial identity (382) he cannot attribute the same importance to humanism as did Lessing, though he recognizes it as an important achievement (378). Humanism, he feels, has been replaced by other, more modern (National Socialist?) ideologies.

In 1941 Benno von Wiese contributed an article on German Enlightenment to a book edited by, among others, Gerhard Fricke. Wiese's interpretation of *Nathan the Wise* strikingly resembles the one given by Fricke. He, too, is unhappy with the play's symbolic and ahistorical setting (Wiese 1941, 253). In Lessing's early works, Wiese remarks, reality and symbolism were successfully united. *Minna von Barnhelm*, for example, achieves a perfect balance between the values of Prussian militarism and Enlightenment, between "Gemeinschaft" and individuality (251). *Nathan the Wise*, on the other hand, marks a tragic turn toward "ethical humanism." Here, Wiese goes even beyond Fricke's assessment. Humanism, he says, proved the downfall of German culture (253).

Some critics wrote fairly objectively about *Nathan the Wise*, the play that National Socialists disliked most, and one may wonder whether this objectivity reflects the writers' intellectual independence during the Third Reich. Rudolf Bach, for example, lists *Nathan the Wise* among Lessing's great works but refrains from making any political comments. He simply refers to the humanism as the central idea behind Lessing's writing (1940, 24 and 30). Oskar Jancke, in the short essay "Über die Prosa Lessings [On Lessing's Prose]" (1940), is mostly interested in finding harmony between Lessing's character and his talent (328). Seemingly in passing, Jancke acknowledges Lessing's fight against fanaticism and intolerance and refers to *Nathan the Wise* in this respect (331). Yet a third critic is unprejudiced against ideas of the Enlightenment such as humanism and tolerance. Paul Fechter quotes passages from *Nathan the Wise* and shows his appreciation for Lessing's personal vision as well as for humanism, one of the major contributions of the eighteenth century ([4]1941, 253). This appreciation is all the more surprising since Fechter, a National Socialist scholar and writer (cf. Wulf 1989, 147f.), praises Hitler's *Mein Kampf* in the same volume (758f.).

b: The "Volksfront"

At the same time as Lessing was being used to represent National Socialist ideals, exiled writers and intellectuals quoted the very same Lessing to denounce Hitler's Germany. In 1933, and in some cases even earlier, communists, socialists, Jews, and liberals had begun to flee their country. They soon formed a unified front, the "Volksfront," in active political opposition to Hitler outside of Germany. That both Nazis and antifascists referred back to a *common* history in their search for ideals, values, and validation did not go unnoticed. Both sides argued that they were the legitimate heirs of their chosen heroes, even if the enemy claimed the same heroes as their own. At a 1935 Volksfront congress in Paris, Heinrich Mann stated that their goal should be the defense of a glorious past and its heritage:

> Wir haben strahlenden Beispielen zu folgen. Wir sind die Fortsetzer und Verteidiger einer großen Überlieferung: Wir, nicht aber die anderen, die den Unterdrückern des Gedankens zu Willen sind oder ihnen Sympathie zeigen. [We have to follow glorious exemplary people. We are the ones who continue and defend a great tradition. We, not the others, who obey and sympathize with those who oppress the thought] (1971, 128).[1]

The question really was — as it would be in the divided postwar Germany — who has the right to represent the "true" Germany? While National Socialists emphasized the national and "Germanic" character of past events, exiled Germany esteemed Humanism and Classicism and looked to developments toward internationalism and emancipation. Wieland Herzfelde, whose journey of exile took him from Prague to Switzerland, London, and finally New York, took a typical stand: Lessing and other historical figures would be dumbfounded by the recent events in Germany, he writes in his article "Wir sollen Deutsch reden [We should speak German]" (1933, 81).

The Volksfront effort was accompanied by attempts to actively keep the German liberal heritage alive. German emigrants in various host countries wrote, read, taught, and performed Germany's culture and art. *Nathan the Wise*, Lessing's least favored play inside Germany during those years, was

---

[1] In 1931, even before Hitler's rise to power, Mann had proposed looking to Lessing as a source of inspiration. Free individuals with a passion to do right have an example in Lessing, Mann told his listeners (458). Lessing always fought for new truths and precipitated changes, be they aesthetic, cultural, or social. Werner Rieck considers Mann's 1931 essay the most important pro-Lessing statement for a bourgeois-humanist perspective (1984, 360).

performed elsewhere more often than any other of his dramas (cf. Berendsohn 1949; Wächter 1973). Before the end of the war, even before the beginning of the Holocaust, parallels were drawn between National Socialist anti-Semitism and the prejudice expressed by the Patriarch in *Nathan*. In the article "Lessings Antwort an Göbbels [Lessing's Answer to Göbbels]" (1936), the communist newspaper *Die Rote Fahne* draws a parallel between the Patriarch's words "Der Jude wird verbrannt [Burn the Jew]" and Hitler's and Göbbels's anti-Jewish sentiments. The same insight is expressed by an article in *Das Wort* one year later. Its author, H.O. Simon, reads *Nathan the Wise* as a "Hohe Lied der Toleranz [Song of Tolerance]" and as a direct attack on the prejudiced National Socialist theory and practice (54). While so many were despairing at the thought that Lessing's warning could not prevent the catastrophe, others gained hope and satisfaction from *Nathan the Wise*. One hundred fifty years of *Nathan the Wise*'s stage history served Julius Bab as proof that a pure and free spirit such as Lessing could survive and be respected in Germany (1944, 262). When World War II was slowly coming to an end, Bab optimistically hoped for a newer, freer Germany that would once again bring *Nathan the Wise* back onto the stage. *Nathan the Wise*, indeed, became the first play produced in postwar Germany.

7: After 1945

a: Reconciliation with the Past

THE END OF THE SECOND World War in 1945 brought with it a renewed interest in *Nathan the Wise*. There was a sense of relief at finding in Lessing a tradition of tolerance of which Germans could be proud. Lessing was quickly rediscovered as a spokesperson for Jewish emancipation, and, more importantly, as a representative of the "better" Germany. Franz Wisten produced *Nathan the Wise* on September 7, 1945, at the Berlin Deutsches Theater. To this day, *Nathan the Wise* has remained one of the most successful plays in the repertory (Diederichsen and Rudin 1980; Stadelmaier 1980, 45; Hasche 1981, 51; Werner 1981, 11; Werner 1984, 408). Critics therefore call it *the* "Wiedergutmachungsdrama [reparation drama]" or "Versöhnungs-Nathan [reconciliation-Nathan]" (Göbel 1977, 263; Stadelmaier 1980, 7; Bohnen 1984, 2). Walter Jens, an important writer and essayist in postwar Germany, writes bitterly that open and hidden anti-Semites alike have used *Nathan the Wise* to furnish themselves with an alibi and to soothe their guilty conscience (1982, 45).

There is another reason why the play was so popular after the war. Jewish actors, upon their return to Germany, reestablished themselves in the artistic community while at the same time making a public statement of their readiness to forgive (cf. Piedmont 1987, 90). Spoken by Jewish actors, Nathan's words of forgiveness toward those who killed his family were particularly powerful to German audiences. Any blatant reference to the Holocaust was avoided, however (Piedmont 1987, 90). It was left to Erwin Piscator to draw this parallel in 1953.[1]

Hermann Kesten speaks for many when he says that looking back on six million murdered Jews, it feels good to be able to point to the one German

---

[1] Piscator interpreted the play as a "Lehrgedicht" (Boeser and Vatkova 1986, 114) intended to instruct the viewers. In his 1953 production of *Nathan the Wise* in Marburg, he used slides and film clips to project statistics and images from the concentration camps. This view of *Nathan the Wise*, one must add, was as unusual in West Germany as in the East. Most Western productions emphasized the comical and conciliatory elements (cf. Stadelmaier 1980, 105; Piedmont 1987, 92).

who spoke out for the Jews long before anyone else did (Kesten 1960, 484). In his opinion "good" Germans may regain some of their self-esteem, and can also learn from Lessing, a thinker, whom Kesten considers a true "moralist" and nonconformist. He sees no contradiction in Lessing having been so unique, on the one hand, and so arch-German ("urdeutsch"), on the other (481).

In her speech accepting the Lessing prize in 1955, Hannah Arendt also grapples with the relationship between recent German history and *Nathan the Wise*. She makes the fine distinction between intolerance as depicted in *Nathan the Wise* and that of modern times (Arendt 1960, 492). Lessing's contemporaries believed that they possessed truth; nowadays people insist that they are right. In either case, she says, the result is fanaticism and an unwillingness to budge from one's convictions. Lessing, who knew that certain values are far more important than any given belief system, would, Arendt asserts, have valued the individual or a friendship more than any theory that asks for human sacrifice, regardless of the theory's scientific validity (492f.). Even if chauvinist beliefs of German racists were true, she says, Nathan teaches us that the individual is human before anything else and needs to be respected as such.

Not every postwar critic believes that *Nathan the Wise* is an exercise in tolerance. Some Jewish writers have raised the point that in the long run, Lessing's play may have had some negative effects. Hans Mayer, for example, does not believe that Lessing did German Jews such a great favor by writing *Nathan the Wise*. In a 1973 article Mayer compares the character of Nathan to Friedrich Schiller's character Spiegelberg (in the early drama *Die Räuber* [The Robbers], 1781) and finds them to be antithetically opposed. Nathan represents the emancipated Jew, whereas Spiegelberg offers the possibility of Jewish messianism (349). Nathan tries to fit in whereas Spiegelberg joins a band of robbers. Neither of them, however, succeeded in replacing the image of Shylock (from Shakespeare's *The Merchant of Venice*), which remained prevalent in Germany and in England (353). Mayer comes to the conclusion that the eighteenth century — including Lessing — was at a loss when it came to harmonizing humanist values and ideals with societal realities (364). Nathan's choice to give up his Jewishness as a national identity was no real alternative for Jews at the time, Mayer holds. Whereas conservative and nationalist writers have sometimes criticized Nathan for being *too* Jewish, Mayer regrets that Nathan's Jewishness remains so abstract and philosophical. Mayer opposes the idea that assimilation was the only solution (352 and 367).[2]

---

[2] Karl S. Guthke steps in to defend Lessing against Mayer's accusations. In a lecture, "Lessing und das Judentum [Lessing and Judaism]" (1976), Guthke argues that Lessing did *not* proclaim assimilation of a few chosen — educated — Jews as the

Unfortunately, he concludes, the Enlightenment could see no further, and neither could Lessing, and neither can today's society, for that matter. The integration of society still depends on the minority's renunciation of its individuality. What presented itself as a choice between assimilation and national identity in 1800 became a choice between Auschwitz or Israel in the twentieth century (363). Mayer's is a powerful argument that interprets *Nathan the Wise* not as an early attempt to counterbalance prejudice and intolerance but rather as the institutionalization of ethnocentrism, which cannot tolerate difference.

Chaim Shoham, in a similar vein, regrets that so many Jews have upheld Lessing as a hero (1980, 25). He regards assimilation, championed in *Nathan the Wise*, as the downfall of West European Judaism. Zionism, on the other hand, could have prevented the Holocaust. It is no coincidence, Shoham argues, that the Eastern Jewry, for the most part believers in Zionism, rejected *Nathan the Wise* (13). One of the examples Shoham gives is Alexander Süskind Rabinovitz, who denied that Lessing's play was useful to the Jewish cause (23f.).

b: Form, Function, Language, and Theology

The western sectors, succeeded in 1949 by the conservative-ruled Federal Republic of Germany, acknowledged responsibility for the Holocaust only hesitatingly. Many literary scholars, accordingly, shied away from anything that might be remotely related to historical or political realities. They occupied themselves with the play's formal or theological aspects and tackled problems such as the function of the parable, and the definition of Lessing's religious legacy.

The debate over that legacy has continued until this day and may well be the one area where opinions will remain the most contradictory (cf. Guthke [3]1979, 87). Immediately after the war Helmut Thielicke and Otto Mann defended Lessing as a loyal and convinced Protestant. Both authors had published during the Nazi era and simply resumed after 1945 where they had

---

solution. Instead, Lessing hoped for *all* Jews to achieve equal legal status (241). Guthke's interpretation, however, neither convinces the reader that Lessing felt strong compassion for the lower- class Jew nor addresses the question whether assimilation per se might not be maladaptive. Another attempt to defend Lessing against Mayer's accusations is made by Ludwig W. Kahn: "Lessing did not wish to assimilate the Jews or integrate them into a German and Christian bourgeoisie" (1986, 243).

left off. Mann, for example, does not write differently in 1948 or 1956 than he did in 1935. Neither does Thielicke, whose *Vernunft und Offenbarung* [Reason and Revelation] (1936 and 1947) was re-edited in 1957 as *Offenbarung, Vernunft und Existenz* [Revelation, Reason and Existence].[3] To do both authors justice, however, it should be stressed that their perspective was a Christian-conservative, not a National Socialist one. Nevertheless, their narrow and conservative interpretation of Lessing as a devout Christian has earned them criticism from their colleagues, and even a moderate critic such as Wolfdiet-rich Rasch notes the "Übermaß an Polemik [excess of polemic]" in Mann's book (Rasch 1956, 553; cf. Barner *et al.* [5]1987, 393).[4]

At first glance, Walter Nigg seems to disagree with Mann and Thielicke. In *Das Buch der Ketzer* [The Book of Heretics] (1949), he first identifies Lessing as one of the most pronounced heretics of the modern age (456). But Nigg then defines heretics as "religious outsiders" who criticize Christianity out of a commitment to improve and advance it (16); he even compares them to saints (19). He is convinced that Lessing was motivated by a deep religious impulse and calls him a founder of new-Protestantism (471ff.). Applying this "insight" to *Nathan the Wise*, Nigg notes that the tolerance preached therein derives from faith, not from indifference. It is only because present times have lost faith that they can no longer understand the true meaning of *Nathan the Wise* (468). Faith, on the other hand, is not identical to religion, and Nigg can understand that Lessing was perplexed by Christian self-righteousness. How could a Christian society have allowed such a "monstrous catastrophe" as the Holocaust to happen, Nigg cannot help but wonder (468).

Karl Barth also believes Lessing to have renewed Protestant theology and calls him one of "the first quite obvious heralds of the programme of Protestant modernism" (1952, 147). Karl Guthke, on the other hand, thinks Lessing belonged to the spiritualistic-mythical tradition of Christianity ([3]1979, 69). Disagreeing with all of these Christian interpretations, Paul Hazard uses the term *Deist* (Hazard 1949). Hans Mayer, finally, associates Lessing with

---

[3] In fact, Thielicke and Mann introduce the postwar editions of their work without giving any reference to recent history. In view of the obvious entanglement of literary studies with Nazi politics (cf. chapter 6), one might have hoped for a bit more self-criticism or at least awareness on the part of the discipline's representatives.

[4] In an unfair attempt to pull to pieces West German criticism as a whole, the East German Anita Liepert limits her examples to Thielicke and Mann as if they represented the full spectrum of West German mainstream criticism (1971, 1327f.; cf. Plavius 1964).

atheism (1953, 284). As is the case with most interpretations, critics frequently tend to look for and find validation of their own ideological positions. The different labels for Lessing's religious conviction may thus fit their creators better than Lessing himself. It comes as a relief, therefore, that more and more scholars admit that no single religious philosophy can be deduced from any of Lessing's works. Johannes Schneider, for example, recognizes that *Nathan the Wise* and the *Erziehung des Menschengeschlechts* reveal outright contradictions (1953, 299). Recently, Eitel Timm has again denied a "einheitliche Richtlinie [uniform guideline]" in Lessing's various works (1989, 35).

The school curricula reflected the apolitical emphasis (cf. König 1974, 443; Barner *et al.* [5]1987, 418-421). Often, textbook annotators fell back on prewar interpretations, not objecting to or even noticing the prejudice of traditional views expressed therein (König 1974, 443f.).

Wolfdietrich Rasch's 1952 interpretation reminds readers of a literary tradition that was interested in foreign cultures — Rasch is thinking of Renaissance authors as well as of Georg Forster, whose *Reise um die Welt* [Trip around the World] had appeared two years prior to *Nathan the Wise*. Rasch does not say a word, however, about recent history, and how these old traditions were being perverted.

The American Germanist Stuart Atkins denies that the parable is central to *Nathan the Wise*. In his article, "The Parable of the Rings in Lessing's 'Nathan der Weise'" (1951), he grants that the parable symbolizes "the brotherhood of man" as well as the necessity of tolerance (267), but he does not believe that it is an adequate answer to Saladin's question. It is inadequate, he explains, because Nathan represents a general Deist humanism, while Saladin is concerned with historical religion. Atkins also acknowledges that Lessing wrote his play shortly before Kant's *Critique of Pure Reason* (1781), in a time, that is, when philosophers began to be discontented with their inability to adequately explain their world and began to ask questions that directly related to reason and the limits of knowledge. Lessing felt this confusion as much as his contemporaries, Atkins says, thus explaining the alleged inconsistencies in the ring parable such as Nathan's inability to answer Saladin's question on a more concrete level.

In his article "La Sagesse de Nathan [The Wisdom of Nathan]" (1955) J.A. Bizet reacted to Klaus Ziegler's comprehensive article on the German drama (1955), which contained one of the first political interpretations of *Nathan the Wise*. Ziegler had claimed that money constitutes a humoristic subplot in the drama (see below, p. 78). There is no subplot, Bizet objects (304). Yes, there are elements of comedy that turn the play into a "Mischspiel [mixed genre]," or a "genre moyen" as Diderot had called it (304f.). The topic of money, however, serves a pragmatic function, according to Bizet. Just as the Bible uses money and gold to symbolize wisdom, so does Lessing bestow Nathan with riches (306). What is really important, Bizet continues, is not that Nathan is rich but rather that he is able to evaluate options, to distinguish right from wrong (307). At the same time, Nathan is generous with his money. This generosity is what differentiates him from the prodigal sultan as well as from the self-denying dervish Al-Hafi (309f.).

Günter Rohrmoser's interpretation of 1958 is primarily interested in structural questions. The play comprises three time dimensions, Rohrmoser finds. Nathan's story begins in the past, the actual plot takes place in the present, and the parable points to the future (118). Rohrmoser acknowledges that the play established iambic verse as Germany's classic meter (121). As far as content is concerned, Rohrmoser does not go beyond any previous interpretation. Behind the play's story and its happy ending, he recognizes the powers of Providence. Providence, he writes, holds the promise for an ideal future, but it is up to the individual to act responsibly so that Providence can take its course (118). Finally, when he characterizes the tone of the drama, Rohrmoser falls back on century-old clichés. What makes Lessing's language so special to him is its "Ton einer männlich überlegenen Gelassenheit [tone of a masculine and superior composure]," 120).

In the third act of *Nathan the Wise*, Recha asks the Templar whether it is true that Mount Sinai is easier to ascend than to descend (Lessing 1970-1979, II 266f.). In his essay "Lessings Parabel von den drei Ringen [Lessing's Parable of the Three Rings]" (1958) Heinz Politzer considers this question to be of vital allegorical importance for the play (343). It is a paradox, he writes, as is Lessing's attempt to convince an audience filled with orthodox opponents of his humanist ideas. To achieve this impossible goal, Lessing wrote the ring parable. But then, what Politzer says about the parable is also somewhat paradoxical. He calls it utopian in tendency (345), but at the same time he detects Kafkaesque elements that anticipate the modern ambivalence toward faith (347). So many vague and paradoxical allusions, he writes, contradict the parable's optimistic message. When the judge scolds the brothers for their selfish behavior and inability to get along, the parable strikes Politzer as a social satire (358). In the end, however, he characterizes it as a classical parable with sacramental undertones (361). Politzer blames Lessing himself for such shifting emphases. An irrational phenomenon such as faith cannot be proven rationally, he holds (357). There are other aspects that irritate Politzer. He wonders if Lessing was not too accommodating of his orthodox viewers. Why else would he have transformed the three "pleasant" sons from Boccaccio's version of the story into three "obedient" ones (350f.)? Politzer overlooks one possible explanation for this decision. If the three sons represent the followers of Judaism, Islam, and Christianity, then Lessing might have wanted to allude to the blind obedience of the religious communities to their leaders. Politzer's criticism of Lessing comes close to dismantling Lessing as the steadfast, heroic, and flawless character he has most often been portrayed as being. Politzer even questions the strength of Lessing's tolerance: had Lessing really been free of prejudice himself, he would not have treated the Christian characters in his play quite as severely (359).

Warren R. Maurer agrees with his American colleague Stuart Atkins. He argues that, on a dramaturgical level, the parable is not well integrated into the play (1962, 54). His article, which appeared first in *Monatshefte* in 1962, suggests that Saladin would have no reason to lay a trap for Nathan by asking his religious opinion when he is really only interested in his money. Maurer therefore doubts that the parable is the centerpiece of the drama. It is merely "an artistic embellishment, a metaphorical statement of what Lessing is trying to say in more concrete terms in the play as a whole" (54). The number three, for example, is introduced in the parable by the three rings and by the three stages of humanity outlined in the judge's sentence (55). In the story surrounding the parable, the number three is important as well. Three characters represent three ideas on three levels: "Nathan symbolizes old age, wisdom, and Judaism. Saladin stands for manhood, despotic reason, and Mohammedanism. And the Tempelherr represents youth, emotionalism, and Christianity" (50). Maurer assumes "a steady threefold progression" from youth to old age and from emotionalism to wisdom (54). He runs into difficulties, however, when he applies this schematism to religion. Even if Judaism is understood as "only incidental to an active, almost pure, humanitarism," it can not be singled out as the "highest" religion without pandering to "the very bigotry against which the play is certainly directed" (56). Not being able to apply the idea of threefold progression to religion, Maurer concludes that Lessing's play exhibits a weakness here. Furthermore, it transgresses "the strict limits of drama." Maybe because he realized these weaknesses, Maurer suggests, Lessing called *Nathan the Wise* "ein dramatisches Gedicht [a dramatic poem]" (56).

Analyzing style and language, the Austrian-born Lessing and Nietzsche scholar Peter Heller draws important conclusions for the philosophical grounding of the work. His *Dialectics and Nihilism* (1966) discusses works by Lessing, Nietzsche, Thomas Mann, and Kafka. The chapter on Lessing deals with *Nathan the Wise* in particular. Heller notes a dialectical principle that governs the style, characters, and action of the play (219). The dialogues, for example, are characterized by frequent interruptions, chains of questions, and repetitions (223). Nathan is the master of the dialectical dialogue: he always succeeds in involving his interlocutor in a truly bilateral discourse (221). He does so especially in the fifth scene of the second act. The Templar's suspicions have been raised against Nathan, and yet Nathan involves him in a dialogue that lets the Templar forget his prejudices and makes him ashamed of having misjudged Nathan even for a moment. Heller also notes that the Patriarch and Daja, the play's most negative characters, are identified by their inability to communicate. They refuse to follow or even listen to other people's arguments, and they deliberately mislead (225). The happy ending of the drama is only possible once all prejudices and secrets are abandoned, and everyone can communicate openly (227).

In his *Die unbefriedigte Aufklärung* [The unsatisfied Enlightenment] (^{2}1979), Willi Oelmüller takes a similar stance to Stuart Atkins's. He lists three reasons why Nathan cannot answer Saladin's question. First, there is no truth as Saladin envisions it. Second, the three religions have long lost their original core. Third, one should not question or criticize the religions, because they are created by God. In short, the problem as posed by Saladin is irrelevant (87). Oelmüller then turns to what he considers the drama's true meaning to be. It lies, he writes, in the judge's advice: accept the tensions and differences in the world, but act ethically (87). This is also what — at least according to Oelmüller's understanding — all three religions demand from their followers. In the end, however, he is skeptical as to how valid this demand is today. Lessing might have believed in the power of religious systems to guide ethical behavior, but in our era, Oelmüller admits regretfully, this may no longer suffice (87). A 1969 article by Belma Emircan expresses a similar sense of ethics, though without the skepticism that plagues Oelmüller. Emircan describes Nathan as a "Homo humanus," a truly humane being who has achieved the highest wisdom: accepting God's will as his own (220).

Michael J. Böhler understands *Nathan the Wise* as a "Spiel vom Grunde [Play about Reason/Cause]" (1971). In the third act Saladin asks for "Gründe [reasons]" that helped Nathan to decide on one religion over the other (Lessing 1970ff., II 2741).[5] In this passage Saladin uses the word *Gründe*

---

[5] One of Saladin's questions may be interpreted falsely by Böhler. Saladin asks "Laß mich die Wahl, die diese Gründe bestimmt.... wissen." Böhler notices that the text says "bestimmt" rather than "bestimmen" and concludes that *Wahl* is the subject: "Let me know the choice that determines the reason" (131). As he admits, this sentence does not make sense. Yet a major part of his essay is based on this reading. What he does not take into account is that Lessing may simply have omitted the conjugated verb for stylistic reasons: "die diese Gründe bestimmt [haben]" — the meaning would then be logical: "Let me know the reasons that determined your

repeatedly and thus brings to mind the principles of classical logic. Obviously, Böhler is thoroughly trained in Greek and Latin rhetoric. He discerns all four types of "causa" in Saladin's question: "causa formalis," "causa materialis," "causa efficiens," and "causa finalis" (132). In each case, "causa" (reason/cause) refers to a different concept: to the material essence of the thing in question, to its historical point of origin, to its essence, or to its goal. Böhler asserts that Nathan refutes one possibility after another in his answer until only the fourth reason is left (133). Böhler calls it the "worum willen" or the "stiftende Grund [foundational reason]." The question can no longer be "where do you come from?" but must be "where are you going" (146)? Nathan himself is an example of such goal-directed orientation. Just as the original ring had the power to bring forth the good, so does Nathan have a "Wille zum Guten [will to do good]" (136). By drawing parallels with Heidegger's terminology (140, 147) — Heidegger also distinguished various types of causes in his work *Vom Wesen des Grundes* — Böhler places Lessing in a larger philosophical context, connecting the classical with the modern period. There can be little doubt that the principles of rhetoric were common knowledge in Lessing's time. It is thus Böhler's merit to have pointed out that layer in *Nathan the Wise* that pertains to classical thought. When he draws parallels to Heidegger, however, Böhler treads on thinner ground. It is always a risky endeavor to reverse the historical process and to read into events or texts what could not have been known at the time.

Helmut Göbel draws on Peter Heller's earlier observations. The title of his book *Bild und Sprache bei Lessing* [Imagery and Language in Lessing's Work] (1971) reveals what he is most interested in: imagery and language. Göbel believes with Heller that language was extremely important to Lessing. In his chapter on *Nathan the Wise*, Göbel characterizes the language and form as "oriental." At the same time, he draws some parallels with biblical language, especially with Jesus' sermons in the New Testament (236, 241). He then examines various metaphors employed by Lessing, such as the unusual plant imagery and the money metaphor.[6] Money plays a particularly important role in Nathan's monologue in scene six of the third act, where Nathan considers how to respond to Saladin's request for truth. He is puzzled: what does the Sultan want from him?

choice" (also cf. Bayard Quincy Morgan's translation in Lessing 1991, 230).

[6] For analyses of other metaphors and images such as fire, water, and plants, cf. Ehrhard Bahr (1974) and Alan D. Latta (1974).

> H'm! h'm! — how strange! — I'm all confused. — What would
> The Sultan have of me? — I thought of money;
> And he wants — truth. Yes, truth! And wants it so—
> So bare and blank — as if the truth were coin! —
> And were it coin, which anciently was weighed! —
> That might be done! But coin from modern mints,
> Which but the stamp creates, which you but count
> Upon the counter — truth is not like that!
> As one puts money in his purse, just so
> One puts truth in his head? Which here is Jew? (Lessing 1991,
>   230)

Peter Demetz (1966) equates the old coin to Nathan's Jewishness, while identifying the new coin with his modern and bourgeois identity. Göbel, on the other hand, wonders whether the old coin may not be more positive than Demetz assumed. It may symbolize, he suggests, the original and true religion. The new coins would then correspond, as do the three rings in the parable, to the new religions: Judaism, Christianity, and Islam (Göbel 1971, 261f.).

Klaus Heydemann turns, once more, to the question whether or not the parable is well integrated into the play. In his contribution to the *Lessing Yearbook* (1975), he answers emphatically in the positive. He reasons that the parable is well introduced by various subplots. The issue between Nathan and the Templar, as well as between Nathan and Saladin, for example, is how conviction is related to deed. This issue is exactly, Heydemann argues, what is at stake in the parable as well (99). The parable also has a dramaturgical function and changes the course of the action. Only *after* Nathan's telling of the story, Heydemann points out, does the play take a different course so that the conflict can be resolved (100f.).

Hendrik Birus's dissertation on *Nathan the Wise*, published in 1978, uncovers an interesting symbolism. He examines the characters' names and finds a deeper meaning in them than has been previously assumed. Birus holds that Lessing deliberately hid the potential meaning of the names. He quotes some of Lessing's own remarks on this topic and reports on the history of "telling names" to prove his point. Birus's argument is that Lessing illustrated Providence's mystical force by choosing names with a cryptic meaning. Even before the blood relation between Recha and the Templar is revealed, their names symbolically express the relationship, thus anticipating Providence.

Hans-Jürgen Schlütter refers in his article "'...als ob die Wahrheit Münze wäre': Zu *Nathan der Weise* III, 6 ['... as if the Truth were a Coin: On *Nathan the Wise*, Scene III, 6]" (1978) to Nathan's monologue about the meaning of truth. Schlütter interprets Nathan's words as follows: the old coin used to be weighed, not counted. The new coins, on the other hand, have only a nominal value. They are counted, not weighed (69). Saladin wants truth as if it were new money, as if it could be counted and owned. The "as if" conjunction is important in Schlütter's eyes. After all, Nathan does not use the comparison *wie,* but the subjunctive *als ob,* indicating that truth is *not* comparable to coins (69). Therefore, Nathan distances himself from the crudely literal attitude evident in Saladin's question (67f.). But what, asks Schlütter, is truth if it is not as freely disposable as money? Schlütter refers to the *Testament Johannis,* a dialogue written by Lessing in 1777. The argument developed in this earlier work is quite similar to the one in *Nathan the Wise,* Schlütter argues (71). Christian love is a value in itself regardless of the confession or religion of any given person (71). This is ultimately the message of *Nathan the Wise* as well, Schlütter says: Nathan embodies pure love. The lay brother recognizes and confirms Nathan's deed by calling him a Christian (72). The truth, Schlütter concludes, does not lie in any particular religion but must be weighed individually.

Robert S. Leventhal is interested primarily in hermeneutics. In his essay "The Parable as Performance: Interpretation, Cultural Transmission and Political Strategy in Lessing's *Nathan der Weise*" (1987) he shows how Lessing's text subverts the hermeneutic assumptions of the eighteenth century. He does so by comparing Lessing's theoretical beliefs to the beliefs of Lessing's time and by testing them against the play. Leventhal's conclusion is a political one: "Lessing placed himself in a political confrontation with religious and state power" (523).

A recent article by Jill Anne Kowalik (1989) offers a psychological reading of the play. She is interested in its "esoteric dimension" and understands the play as Lessing's reaction to tragic losses in his own life. His wife, Eva, died on January 10, 1778, only a couple of weeks after the couple had lost their newborn son. Kowalik points out that in *Nathan the Wise* "the main figures react to the loss of a close relative or spouse"(2). Nathan lost his family; Saladin and Sittah lost their brother. A novel aspect of her analysis is her assertion that Nathan and the Patriarch can be viewed as split aspects of the same figure. Whereas the Patriarch resembles Lessing's critical and intolerant father, Nathan is "the father Lessing wanted but never got: the man who loves his child regardless of differences over religious orthodoxy" (12f.).

More recently, Rolf Simon has again pointed to the play's rhetorical element. The abstract of his essay "Nathans Argumentationsverfahren [Nathan's method of argumentation]" (1991) emphasizes "that Lessing's theories require an act of transformation into the dramatic simulation of intersubjectivity. Thus, *Nathan der Weise* can be read as both, a confirmation and a critique of Lessing's theories" (609). Simon's provocative thesis is that two characters in the play, the dervish and the Patriarch, remain immune to Nathan's rhetorical skills. It must be added, however, that Nathan never tries to talk Al-Hafi, the dervish, out of his trip to the Ganges, nor does Nathan ever meet with the Patriarch face to face. Nevertheless, the fact remains that Nathan's influence is limited. By acknowledging the limits of the power of language, Simon holds, Lessing integrated a critique of his communicative model into the play (633).

c: Utopia

Jürgen Schröder understands *Nathan the Wise* primarily as a utopian play. His *Gotthold Ephraim Lessing: Sprache und Drama* [Gotthold Ephraim Lessing: Language and Drama] (1972) extends some of the explorations begun by Peter Heller (1966) and Helmut Göbel (1971). As we saw earlier (pp. 69-72), Heller and Göbel both stress the importance of dialectics in Lessing's writing. In the same vein, Schröder calls *Nathan the Wise* a "Drama der Verständigung," a play of understanding and/or communication. Comparing the final version of *Nathan the Wise* to a surviving rough draft, Schröder illustrates Lessing's continuous efforts to improve the dialectical structures of his dialogues (275-283). Nathan is as much a master of language as is his creator Lessing. Both, Schröder explains, place their trust in the spoken word while pursuing their mission of communication and education (253). Drawing such a close connection between communication and education, Schröder emphasizes the play's didactic elements. He considers Nathan a born teacher and the play itself a "Lehrstück." The play's ultimate message, according to Schröder, is a utopian state in which communication will be free of misunderstanding and prejudice (248 and 263). This message becomes clear in the play's final scene, where the happy family tableau symbolizes such a state. Whereas other critics have expressed discomfort with the drama's unrealistic ending, Schröder believes it to be the play's logical consequence (258). True communication as exercised by Nathan will lead to utopia, Schröder suggests. Of course, he is aware that history, especially Germany's history, has been a drama of miscommunication and senselessness (268). All the more reason, Schröder concludes, why Lessing's utopian model of communication should be reconsidered (268).

Another attempt to establish *Nathan the Wise* as a utopian vision is made by Hinrich Seeba in his book on *Die Liebe zur Sache* [The Love for a Cause] (1973). Whereas Schröder's utopia was based on free communication, Seeba's ideal involves love and moderation. Moderation is necessary because without it, fanaticism would unleash its destructive force. Seeba has no sympathy for "causes," be they political, patriotic, or moral, and argues that Lessing felt the same. This hostility to causes is why all of Lessing's plays criticize, according to Seeba, a particular cause and its exaggerating devotees. The aim of *Nathan the Wise*, Seeba writes, is to expose the insatiable desire of the church for power. The character who most fanatically fights for this cause is the Patriarch (101). The Patriarch, Seeba feels, represents the desire for power and political control much more than any particular religion or Christian belief (101ff.). With his senseless repetition of the words "Der Jude wird verbrannt," he represents a type of fanaticism that, Seeba believes, is responsible for the evil in the world. The Patriarch, in his unconditional devotion to a cause, leads directly to Max Weber and from there to Adolf Hitler (122). Had Lessing's utopia prevailed, and had the world learned to remain suspicious of fanaticism, Seeba seems to suggest, the Third Reich could have been prevented.

The excellent handbook *Lessing: Epoche — Werk — Wirkung* [Lessing: Epoch - Work - Response] (^{5}1987), co-edited by Wilfried Barner, Gunter Grimm, Helmuth Kiesel (who is largely responsible for the chapter on *Nathan the Wise*), and Martin Kramer, has been revised and updated several times since its initial publication in 1975. The editors present the latest trends in criticism and do not refrain from giving their own interpretation. In the case of *Nathan the Wise*, they look at the various ways the play has been interpreted and accept the utopian view as *one* of the play's aspects. According to them, the last scene might be understood as Lessing's illustration of a concept he had introduced earlier. In his *Erziehung des Menschengeschlechts* [*The Education of the Human Race*], the authors remind their readers, Lessing had prophesied the coming of a "Drittes Evangelium [a new eternal gospel]" (318, cf. G.E. Lessing 1991, 332). They quickly admit, however, that the utopia is presented at the price of a loss in reality. Maybe to draw attention to the discrepancy between utopian ideal and societal realities, Lessing invented Al-Hafi, a counterbalance to Nathan's optimism (331f.).

As the title of his *Natürlichkeit und Wirklichkeit* (1976) indicates, Dominik von König identifies in Lessing's *Nathan the Wise* the ideal state of "Natürlichkeit [naturalness]" opposed to a flawed "Wirklichkeit [reality]." In the play they are set off against one another: Nathan embodies the ideal state while the Patriarch represents reality. The difference becomes obvious, König holds, when one analyzes the language and rhetoric each character uses. Confirming Schröder's analysis of the action of the play as taking place *within* language, König examines individual dialogues and scenes to make his point. The Patriarch uses the inhuman language of reality. Driven by the hunger for power, it reduces people to their roles, it employs "tote Zeichen" (dead signs) instead of words relating to human concepts (136). In the beginning, Saladin too speaks the Patriarch's language. When he asks Nathan for "truth," he is using a dead sign. Nathan, who thinks and talks differently, cannot answer (109). Nathan uses the language of naturalness. He overturns dead signs and prejudices; he recognizes people as individuals (139). This position is expressed, for example, in his response to the Templar, who has just accused the Jews of fancying themselves a chosen people:

> Ha! You know not how much closer
> I now shall cling to you. — O come, we must,
> We must be friends! — disdain my folk, as much
> As ever you will. For neither one has chosen
> His folk. Are we our folk? What is a folk?
> Are Jew and Christian sooner Jew and Christian
> Than man? How good, if I have found in you
> One more who is content to bear the name
> Of man! (Lessing 1991, 214)

Somewhere between the two extremes is Al-Hafi, who criticizes the "real" world but also doubts the validity of Nathan's utopian vision (65). With the ring parable, Nathan converts Saladin to "natural" communication (141). He breaks through Saladin's "falsches Bewußtsein [false consciousness]." The ring parable finally convinces Saladin that language and thought are not commodities. Nathan teaches him the values of naturalness: knowledge of other people, communication, and responsible action. As König points out, three examples of responsible actions have already taken place by the time the play begins, resulting in the saving of lives (Nathan has adopted Recha, Saladin has let the Templar go free, and the Templar has saved Recha from the fire).[7] These actions made it possible for Providence to take its course, leading to the family reunion at the end (27). König interprets the last scene as a sketch of a better world, a utopia that demonstrates to the readers how the world should be and what needs to be done to get there (18).[8]

---

[7] Helmut Fuhrmann adds the observation that all three deeds transgress religious boundaries: the Jew adopts a Christian, the Moslem pardons a Christian, and the Christian rescues a Jew (1983, 64).

[8] Even though König acknowledges the didactic aspect of the play, he rejects the term *Lehrstück* (179).

Without explicitly referring in his interpretation to a utopian vision, Peter Horst Neumann seems to lean toward such a view. In *Der Preis der Mündigkeit* [The Price of Coming of Age] (1977), Neumann concentrates on one central theme in all of Lessing's plays: How can reason justify authority in an enlightened society (6)? Lessing's fathers illustrate the various possible positions of authority, Neumann argues. Sir William Samson (in Lessing's first tragedy, *Miss Sara Sampson*) is a benevolent father; Odoardo Galotti (in *Emilia Galotti*) is a father who abused his power. With Nathan, however, Lessing finally created the "ideal" father.[9] Nathan is not Recha's natural father (61), but he has *earned* his role as father, a fact that makes his position even more legitimate. Neumann notes that in the play's last scene Saladin also claims to be a father to Recha and the Templar. That Lessing bestows Saladin at that moment with material wealth (his caravans laden with treasures and money finally arrive) indicates to Neumann that at that point Lessing considered Saladin worthy of his new father role. Gold in fairy tales usually symbolizes kindness, Neumann explains, and Lessing provides his better father figures with it (67f.). The Patriarch is the third father figure in the play, according to Neumann. If Nathan is a perfected Sampson, then the Patriarch is Odoardo Galotti taken to an extreme.[10] The term "Anti-Father" (69) is certainly fitting to describe the Patriarch, but perhaps Neumann does not take the Patriarch seriously enough. He compares the play to a fairy tale (72), thus ridding the Patriarch of real destructive power (evil is always conquered in fairy tales). Neumann concludes his analysis by envisioning a utopian "Mündigwerden [coming of age]" of mankind. Sons will in time turn into fathers (what about women?) and will earn the role by realizing the principles of goodness, love, and reason (74).

Recently, Eitel Timm has examined *Nathan the Wise* once more. His book *Ketzer und Dichter. Lessing, Goethe, Thomas Mann und die Postmoderne in der Tradition des Häresiegedankens* [Heretic and Poet: Lessing, Goethe, Thomas Mann and Post Modernism in the Tradition of Heretic Thought] (1989) places Lessing in the tradition of religious and political heretics. Timm

[9] Nathan as an exceptional father figure is also discussed in Karin Wurst's *Familiale Liebe ist die "wahre Gewalt". Die Repräsentation der Familie in G.E. Lessings dramatischem Werk* (1988, 148-169).

[10] As is the case with most of Lessing's dramas, the interpretation of *Emilia Galotti* has undergone considerable changes in the last decades. Neumann sees Odoardo Galotti, Emilia's father, no longer as a bourgeois hero but as a moralistic fanatic and the murderer of his daughter.

argues convincingly that Lessing's oppositional convictions are in direct contradiction to the utopian tradition (43).

d: The Bourgeois Element

Especially since the 1960s, Lessing has been considered a bourgeois and democratic writer.[11] Likewise, *Nathan the Wise* has been understood as a play of bourgeois values. Nathan is not only a Jew, after all: he is also a merchant. One of the first critics to note the important role that money plays in *Nathan the Wise* was Klaus Ziegler (1955). Money, he suggests, is at the center of a humoristic subplot that runs through the play, creating tension and qualifying the mostly idealistic tone of the play (2111). By pairing ethical with sociological concerns and by introducing the theme of money into an idealistic play, Lessing anticipated the future, Ziegler writes (2100 and 2113).

Cesare Cases takes this interpretation a step further (1963). He refers to the "coin metaphor" (from Nathan's monologue quoted above, p. 72) and argues that Nathan instinctively distinguishes truth from money because of the double role he has in the play. He is not only the patient Jew; he is also the cunning businessman (332). Cases thus opens the door to a reevaluation of Nathan's character. Despite his materialistic interpretation, however, Cases also maintains that the final scene symbolizes utopian harmony (337).

Peter Demetz concludes his 1966 paperback edition of *Nathan the Wise* with an essay on the historical and dramaturgical aspects of the play. He, too, notes Nathan's double role and even considers him caught between these two identities as between two sets of rules: the bourgeois and the Jewish. At first, however, Demetz compares Lessing's dramatic theory to Diderot's (as Bizet did before him). Believing in the theater's obligation to represent life, Diderot objected to an artificial distinction between the sad and the comic. Demetz argues that Lessing shared Diderot's view and mixed genres freely. Thus, he says, *Nathan the Wise* is best described as a "serious comedy" (169, 173) since it is as much a true comedy as is *Minna von Barnhelm* (178).

At the same time, Demetz detects elements in *Nathan the Wise* of the eighteenth-century sentimental family drama that originated in England but was prevalent in Germany as well. Because Lessing so deliberately mixes

---

[11] This is the prevailing interpretation today. A recent book by Peter Michelsen discussing Lessing, for example, carries the title *Der unruhige Bürger* [The Restless Bourgeois] (1990).

styles and genres, he sometimes has to take liberties with style — this is how Demetz explains flaws in the play's meter. Lessing uses iambic verse to create an Oriental atmosphere, but then he interrupts its flow, disintegrates and almost destroys the meter so as to give his viewers and readers a chance to recognize their own colloquial language (181). This interpretation attributes to Lessing a rather modern intention, and indeed, Demetz suggests that Lessing's almost stenographic rendering of colloquial German anticipates the "Sekundenstil" of later periods (184).

As far as content is concerned, Demetz concentrates on the three male characters and what they represent. He sees Saladin, Sultan and historical figure, as an exponent of world history. On a more private level, Saladin is also a father as well as a son — an observation that escaped most critics before Demetz. The Patriarch recalls the Enlightenment's vigorous theological disputes. Nathan embodies the individual's right to private religion (169). Nathan is, of course, a Jew, but even more, Demetz asserts, he is a middle-class bourgeois (200ff.). Demetz holds that Nathan only plays the role of a Jew, barely identifying with his religion (209). Had he decided and taken a stand, he might have been able to answer Saladin's question. As he is on the junction of two paths, however, he cannot satisfy Saladin. Demetz concludes that Saladin's problem remains unsolved — and the "key" to the drama is still missing (204).

From this point on, the image of Nathan as a bourgeois is commonplace among critics. Paul Hernadi refers to it in the title of his article in the *Lessing Yearbook:* "Nathan der Bürger: Lessings Mythos vom aufgeklärten Kaufmann [Nathan as Bourgeois: Lessing's Myth of the Enlightened Merchant]" (1971). Hernadi shows how Nathan's, similar to the judge's, position anticipates Weber's economic theory and the Protestant work ethic. That individuals have to *earn* their privileges, that hard work and diligence will lead to fulfillment, that success is proof of God's favoritism — these are ideas, Hernadi writes, that apply to Lessing's play as much as to the Protestant work ethic (346). Hernadi notes that Lessing developed such ideas ten years *before* the French Revolution established the notion that privileges should be accessible to everybody or nobody. It certainly makes sense to see Nathan as a representative of the rising bourgeois class. What is questionable about Hernadi's interpretation is that it presents the economic layer as the only one in the play. Consequently, Hernadi is not happy with Lessing's choice of a medieval Jew as protagonist. A modern-day German merchant would have served the purpose better, Hernadi finds (348f.).

In his *Der Bürger als Held* [The Bourgeois as Hero] (1973), Heinz Schlaffer follows the emergence of the "bourgeois hero" in literature. In his chapter on *Minna von Barnhelm* (86-125) he frequently refers to *Nathan the Wise*. By a sociohistorical analysis he shows how Nathan expresses the self-confidence characteristic of the bourgeois class at the end of the eighteenth century. It was, Schlaffer writes, the bourgeoisie who newly possessed financial power and therefore demanded to be considered as on the same level as the king, represented in *Nathan the Wise* by Saladin (107).[12] Schlaffer sees further proof of his theory in the ring parable. In the old days the ring, like aristocratic titles and privileges, was passed down to the oldest son. This "tyranny" was replaced by the new bourgeois laws. As the judge explains in the story, the ring will no longer be automatically inherited but must be earned (109f.) Schlaffer is especially impressed that Lessing not only *described* the new economic law but also warned his readers — by way of Al-Hafi — of the danger that lies in taking the accumulation of money as a goal in itself (116f.). Al-Hafi leaves his job as treasurer in Saladin's court towards the end of Act 2. He objects to Saladin's politics and the subjugation of people for financial reasons. Fleeing a corrupt world, he opts for a life of seclusion on the Ganges.

Karl Eibl (1981) addresses the religious question, social aspects as well as actual historical references in the play, the sociological problem of power and how to legitimize it, and, finally, the importance *Nathan the Wise* might have for the bourgeois identity. Lessing is, Eibl proclaims, *the* poet of bourgeois society. The bourgeois struggle for consensus and adaptability are anticipated by Lessing (27). In fact, Eibl argues, the lesson Lessing wanted to convey in *Nathan the Wise* was that consensus is possible and that differences can be overcome (27). Because to him Lessing's intention was so obviously educational, Eibl calls the play a didactic parable (7). The final scene, he writes, illustrates this point. Nevertheless, Eibl hesitates to classify the play as utopian. The happy ending did not come easily, Eibl writes, and it could have been catastrophic (26). Eibl's glorification of bourgeois society and its achievement of consensus, however, apparent especially toward the end of his essay, gives his interpretation an optimistic if not actually utopian flavor.

e: Lessing and Brecht

Some recent newspaper articles have taken for granted that Bertolt Brecht, the inventor of Marxist and dialectical theater, must be seen as Lessing's successor

---

[12] Cf. Ziegler, who paralleled the Sultan's low cash flow to the inability of eighteenth-century courts to support themselves (1955, 2112).

(Schütt 1979, 19; Raddatz 1981, 41).[13] Whether he is or not has been debated by Lessing critics. Paolo Chiarini (1957) and Hans-Joachim Schrimpf (1965) agree that he is. They notice some striking similarities in both authors' theoretical approaches to the theater. Schrimpf points out some commonalities (8ff.): the interest both had in educating their audience and the polemical style that they shared, their preoccupation with political theater, as well as their curiosity to try out new approaches, techniques, and stage effects. Both writers, Schrimpf elaborates, antagonized conservatives (15) and were therefore often criticized.

Reinhold Grimm asks in his 1974 contribution to the *Lessing Yearbook*: "Lessing — Ein Vorläufer Brechts? [Lessing — A Predecessor of Brecht?]" (1974). He warns not to overestimate the "striking similarities" between the two writers. Lessing's "Versuche [experiments]" he argues, are different from Brecht's "Versuche" (37). While Lessing wanted his viewers to feel "Mitleid [pity]" for the characters, Brecht was concerned with breaking the dramatic illusion of reality (42).[14] On the other hand, Grimm admits that both playwrights wanted to educate, promoting the didactic function of the theater (41). His conclusion is that Brecht was not a direct follower of Lessing, but that he knew, respected, and renewed certain aspects of Lessing's work (45). Grimm also, however, considers there to be some "astonishing correspondences" (52f.) between *Nathan the Wise* and Brecht's *Kaukasische Kreidekreis* [Caucasian Chalk Circle]. Taken from the Bible, Brecht's story involves two women who fight the right to care for a baby. A judge gives the baby back to the biological mother because she refused to do violence to the child to win him back. Her love thus put the well-being of the child first. In both plays the judges have comparable functions, Grimm explains, and each has a certain messianic and utopian dimension. The mixture of comedy and tragedy in *Nathan the Wise*, Grimm concludes, corresponds to the theory of Brecht's "Lehrtheater [didactic theater]" (49).

The comparison between Lessing's *Nathan the Wise* and Brecht's *Kaukasische Kreidekreis* is taken a step further in Richard Critchfield's essay "The Mixing of Old and New Wisdom" (1982). He finds some astounding

---

[13] Raddatz presents a *triumvirate* of men who follow Lessing: Marx, Freud, and Brecht.

[14] It is not quite fair of Grimm to overlook the fact that Schrimpf saw the difference. Schrimpf's view was that Lessing wanted his viewers to identify with the actor onstage only as a person distinct from him- or herself. Lessing's viewers were to process what they experienced and to integrate it in their lives. In a way, Schrimpf remarks, this goal is not so different from what Brecht had in mind (1965, 45).

similarities between the plays. Both "depict the world not only as it is, but also as Lessing and Brecht believed it should be" (164). The Bible reader will also recognize traces of the story of the good Samaritan. *Nathan the Wise* and *Der kaukasische Kreidekreis* anticipate "a future age whose fulfillment is alluded to in the play's utopian landscape (168). Both plays end with the characters embracing one another. "Such parallels are more than merely coincidental," Critchfield writes (168). He does not, however, intend "to describe Brecht as a poet who plagiarized Lessing's famous play," especially since Lessing himself was indebted to other authors. Critchfield merely speaks "of Brecht's own affinity for the great enlightener" (172).

Wilfried Barner and his co-editors of *Lessing: Epoche — Werk — Wirkung* see the parallels as well. Like Grimm, however, they warn not to carry the comparison between Brecht and Lessing too far. After all, they write, Lessing was part of the very bourgeois theater of illusion that Brecht tried to surpass ([5]1987, 315f.).

f: The East German Criticism

The question of literary heritage, discussed before 1945 by communists and exiled intellectuals, remained of paramount importance in East Germany after the war. The German Democratic Republic looked back on history searching for those cultural figures and writers who could in any way be considered part of a humane, antifascist, or revolutionary tradition (cf. Zimmermann 1985, 322). Lessing fit this description since his dramas could easily be interpreted as contributions to the bourgeois struggle against aristocratic and clerical authorities (Barner *et al.* [5]1987, 422).

Lessing criticism in East Germany reinstated Franz Mehring's *Lessing-Legende* as its reference point for analysis. Mehring's thesis that Lessing had an authentic class instinct and class consciousness was further developed by Paul Rilla. Rilla's *Lessing und sein Zeitalter* [Lessing and his Time], published first in 1958, quickly became the authoritative biography (1973).[15] Like Mehring before him, Rilla sees in Lessing the forerunner of socially conscious literature. He is interested both in Lessing's philosophical and aesthetic writ-

---

[15] The East German critic Hans-Georg Werner is not quite happy with the authority Mehring's and Rilla's books achieved in the East. He holds that Mehring's influence obstructed critics from finding new access to Lessing's work (1984, 404). Rilla's interpretation, Werner comments, is unrealistic and mystifies Lessing.

ings. The religious disputes are interpreted as "antitheological" and, therefore, as revolutionary acts (433, 445). Because both Mehring and Rilla saw Lessing only in the frame of a materialistic philosophy which focused on the issue of class struggle, they could not really do justice to Lessing's literary work. Hans-Georg Werner accuses the East German Lessing criticism of continuing this trend (1981, 15; 1984, 412, 424). Wolfgang Albrecht, another East German critic who comments on his colleagues' contributions to Lessing criticism, is more positive. One year before German unification, he acknowledges some shallowness in Marxist criticism but puts it above West German criticism in its truthfulness (1990, 1165f.).

At the center of most East German criticism is the question of Lessing's political significance. One of the critics who value Lessing as a theoretical source for Marxism-Leninism is Anita Liepert (1971, 1318). She specifically identifies the concepts of pantheism, dialectics, and materialism in Lessing's work (1319f.). Thomas Höhle emphasizes Lessing's importance for working-class culture (1984, 279). Dieter Heinemann, on the other hand, denies such an influence (1984, 365). Claus Träger (1976) is mostly interested in Lessing's critical work. He describes him as a bourgeois author who stood at the beginning of a development which would eventually lead to the German Democratic Republic (92). Träger's assessment of Lessing as a writer who must be seen in the framework of a slowly emerging bourgeois society is not so different from that of his West German colleagues except for his implication that communist East Germany was the natural heir to this bourgeois society. Hans-Georg Werner's view (1984) is that Lessing's intellectual and moral stance might be considered bourgeois, but not his political philosophy. Lessing is historically significant, explains Werner, because his world view eventually ran counter to exploitative interests (439).

Besides the debate on Lessing's "bourgeois" status, East German critics were interested in his reception. Contributions to the frequent Lessing conferences often dealt with Lessing's literary influence on proletarian institutions or Eastern European cultures. Hans-Georg Werner (1980) and the faculty at Humboldt University (1982), for example, published books that concentrate on this aspect.

As far as *Nathan the Wise* was concerned, Marxist scholars were initially not much interested. Even though the play was widely performed, literary critics such as Mehring and Lukács hardly referred to it (cf. Lützeler 1971, 181). Paul Rilla (1973), who praises *Emilia Galotti* above all, barely even mentions *Nathan the Wise*. The few critics who interpret *Nathan the Wise* understand it as a play directed against absolutism. An example of this interpretation is Günter Hartung's analysis of *Nathan the Wise* as "Gesellschaftskritik [social criticism]" (1984, 165). Al-Hafi's verbal protest against Saladin's fiscal policies is of particular importance to Hartung. Through Al-Hafi, Hartung says, Lessing criticized the exploitative politics of absolute monarchy (165). Hartung also looks at the reception of *Nathan the Wise* and condemns attacks on the play such as those by the National Socialist as attacks directed at the proletariat (173).

East German educators stressed the political and antifeudal elements in Lessing's writing. Teachers were advised to have students compare the humanism expressed in *Nathan the Wise* with the Socialist conception of humanism (Barner *et al.* [5]1987, 423). On stage, Friedo Solters's 1966 production of *Nathan the Wise* was the most influential (cf. Stadelmaier 1980, 176). The twist in this interpretation is that Saladin, the feudal ruler, is the villain, while the Patriarch plays only a minor role. The political and historical approaches to a new understanding of Lessing in the East fell back on some of the same clichés used by previous critics. One example is Inge von Wangenheim, who praises Lessing's character in the following way: "Das Beste an ihm für alle Zeiten war, ist und bleibt er selbst. Er war ein Charakter [The best thing about him was, is, and will be himself, for all times. He was a character]" (1981, 172).

g: Lessing and the Consequences

As literary critics have become more interested in reception theory and the history of criticism, Lessing's reception has become the focus of recent scholarly works — including this one. Many books have appeared that put together examples of Lessing criticism (Bauer 1968; Steinmetz 1969; Daunicht 1971; Steinmetz 1979; Dvoretzky 1981; Henning 1981; Bohnen 1982; Bohnen 1984). Going beyond the mere presentation of historical documents, scholars have addressed the question of the significance of Lessing for German intellectual history. Has he contributed to political progress or did he, perhaps unintentionally, pander to reactionary tendencies? Was he a revolutionary, or a conservative, or maybe a mixture of both? Was *Nathan the Wise* not read before 1933 by the same people who would later participate in the Holocaust (cf. Hildebrandt 1990, 461)? What can today's readers learn from the work?

Hans Mayer equates Lessing's credo with the interest of the bourgeois class (1953). He notes, however, that Lessing's thinking had little effect on his fellow Germans. This is also the thesis of Peter Demetz's article "Die Folgenlosigkeit Lessings [Lessing's Lack of Effect]" (1971). It is therefore not clear why Demetz sets out to refute Mayer's essay. Both authors also agree on

Lessing's indebtedness to Diderot. Where Demetz differs from Mayer is in his political evaluation of Lessing. Demetz, who does not share Mayer's Marxist perspective, considers Lessing's political convictions to have been "conservative revolutionary." For his time, however, Lessing was too revolutionary. Demetz argues that Germans behaved differently from the French, choosing to escape reality rather than change it. Thus, they turned their backs on Lessing and the Enlightenment, embracing Classicism instead. While the French made a revolution, the Germans committed themselves to Idealist philosophy and religious conservatism (731ff.).

Horst Steinmetz, on the other hand, finds that Lessing has been relevant for the last two hundred years, now maybe more than ever (1977, 14). His essay "Gotthold Ephraim Lessing: Aktualität eines umstrittenen Klassikers [Gotthold Ephraim Lessing: Timeliness of a Controversial Classical Writer]," originally conceived as a lecture for the 1976 Lessing conference in Cincinnati, notes that every historical period has claimed "its" Lessing, while at the same time refuting every previous attempt to interpret him (15). Steinmetz commented on the ever-present apologetic tone of most Lessing criticism some years earlier in the introduction to his *Lessing — ein unpoetischer Dichter* [Lessing — an Unpoetic Poet] (1969, 14).[16] While Steinmetz's point is well taken, Demetz's argument is also convincing. That critics have always claimed to understand Lessing does not say anything about the effect Lessing's work has had.

Barner and his co-editors of the handbook *Lessing. Epoche — Werk - Wirkung* (^{5}1987) observe that Lessing was not a political activist in the modern sense (346). They grant him, however, "kritische[s] Problembewußtsein [a critical awareness of political problems]" that has inspired some of his readers to question certain of his positions and viewpoints (346). That the reactions he provoked have been so ideological ("die ausgesprochen ideologischen Interpretationen"), however, brings them in the epilogue to their handbook to agree with Demetz's thesis that Lessing has been of no consequence to Germany's intellectual history (427).

Josef Schnell commends Lessing's play as a didactic exercise for literature classes in his article "Dramatische Struktur und soziales Handeln: Didaktische

---

[16] Steinmetz himself, however, follows a similar agenda and tries to rehabilitate Lessing by correcting earlier misconceptions about him. How else could his warning not to turn Lessing into the other, better German (1969, 44) and *not* to associate him with philo-Semitism be understood: "Man verkennt seine Intentionen und seine Ausgangsposition gründlich, bringt man ihn in irgendeiner Form mit einem Philosemitismus in Verbindung" (44f.).

Überlegungen zur Lektüre von Lessings 'Nathan der Weise' [Dramatic Structures and Social Action: Didactic Deliberations on the Reading of Lessing's 'Nathan the Wise']" (1976). The play offers the student a chance to learn how to evaluate the relationship between literature and history, as well as how to think for himself or herself. The classical play may not be able to answer today's problems, Schnell writes, but it illustrates the development of problems throughout history (471).

Gerhard Bauer is not happy with critics who belittle the political implications of Lessing's work. In an essay tellingly entitled "Revision von Lessing's 'Nathan' [Revision of Lessing's 'Nathan']" (1976), he singles out Hinrich Seeba and accuses him of defusing the importance of Lessing and the Enlightenment (74f.). Bauer's interpretation does not shy away from making political references. He understands Saladin as a complex character who bears some resemblance to Frederick the Great. Both monarchs, Bauer explains, had positive as well as negative character traits, and Lessing depicted this ambiguity well (85). Bauer also draws a parallel between the Patriarch and the American CIA (93). His perspective is clearly class-conscious. He understands *Nathan the Wise* as an expression of bourgeois class interests: there is the struggle against absolutism and feudalism (92), on the one hand, and the vision of a united bourgeoisie, on the other hand (101). Bauer stays clear of the trap, however, of reading too much into Lessing's work. He acknowledges Lessing's religious loyalty and excuses this conservative twist to Lessing's philosophy as rooted in its historical context. Lessing was no "Bravheits-apostel [apostle of good behavior]," Bauer concludes his argument, but then he did not come close to the materialist maturity of his French counterparts either (99).

Wilm Pelters, on the other hand, does not believe that Lessing was a "political writer" (1977, 251). His article on *Nathan the Wise* as "Anti-Candide oder die Apotheose der Vorsehung [Anti-Candide or Apotheoses of Providence]" culminates in the provocative thesis that Lessing's play is inherently conservative. Pelters thus holds Lessing responsible for reactionary trends in Germany and maybe even for Hitler's genocide. This is, of course, the same argument that Hans Mayer made in 1973 (see above, pp. 64f.). In *Lessings Standort* [Lessing's Position] (1972) Pelters demonstrated that Lessing had expressed in *Nathan the Wise* an optimistic belief in human and historical progress. Pelters's conclusion is convincing, even though he fumbles when it comes to interpreting the role of the Patriarch.[17] What is really pertinent in Pelter's argument is his assertion that an optimistic belief in Providence bears the risk of passivity, if not resignation (1972, 108).[18] It is this thought that Pelters develops in his 1977 article. Pelters argues that Lessing's belief in Providence might have led to Herder, Hegel, and Marx, but it also led to the ethical paralysis that spawned the concentration camps (1977, 253ff.). Other writers of his time — Pelters mentions French authors such as Voltaire — were much more progressive than Lessing. Pelter's interpretation at this point draws on Mendelssohn's verdict, calling *Nathan the Wise* an "Anti-Candide" (Mendelssohn 1785, 143). Pelters seems to have a point: while Voltaire in his *Candide* faced the fact that the world is an arbitrary place, Lessing took, intellectually, a step back.

Klaus Bohnen, too, applies a political reading to Lessing's work and to *Nathan the Wise* in particular (Bohnen 1979). His perspective, though, is a moderate one. Taking a fresh look at the final scene of *Nathan the Wise*, Bohnen interprets the play as a "Gegenbild einer Gesellschaft [an alternative view of society]" (383). To prove his thesis, he relies on Lessing's *Ernst und Falk*. Bohnen contrasts the discussion of society in the philosophical dialogues of Ernst and Falk (written in 1778-1780) to the model of society that is practically realized in *Nathan the Wise* (378). In both works, Bohnen elaborates, Lessing expresses the need for the individual to become a responsible member of society and to act according to reason and nature (390f.). Because Bohnen assumes that Lessing really wanted the individual to change, he does not interpret Lessing's "model" as a utopia. Instead, he describes Lessing's vision as "gesellschaftsemanzipativ, zugleich jedoch staatsbewahrend [socially emancipatory, yet politically conservative]" (401). In a later book, *Lessing: Nachruf auf einen Aufklärer* [Lessing: Necrology of an Enlightener] (1982), Bohnen considers what modern German society has learned from Lessing. Many recent West German critics, he finds, use Lessing

---

[17] Pelters does not follow Maurer, who, as we have seen (p. 69), referred to the Templar, Saladin, and Nathan as representatives of young, middle, and old age (1962, 50). Instead, Pelters chooses Daja, the Patriarch, and Nathan to symbolize stages in human development — a questionable interpretation, as Pelters realizes (72).

[18] This argument is not so different from what Horkheimer and Adorno said in their *Dialektik der Aufklärung* [Dialectic of the Enlightenment] (1947). They blamed Enlightenment for regressive developments in German history. There is some doubt whether the authors would have actually included Lessing in their argument, since they never mention him directly (cf. A. Heller 1987, 31).

to promote the idea of tolerance and pluralism; once more, critics are using Lessing to justify their own view of the world (180). One must consider, however, that commemorative articles — Bohnen quotes newspaper articles written for the two hundredth anniversary of Lessing's death in 1981 — always exaggerate the harmonious aspects of the topic at hand.

In her *Lessings "Nathan der Weise" und sein Leser: Eine wirkungs-ästhetische Studie* [Lessing's 'Nathan the Wise' and its Readers: A reception aesthetic Study] (1980) Sigrid Suesse-Fiedler compares the reception of *Nathan the Wise* to the responses Lessing intended to achieve. She reduces the past reception of the play to three schools of thought: the biographical-historical approach of critics such as Benno von Wiese and Hermann Hettner, anti-Semitic interpretations, and "werkimmanent [autonomous]" criticism that analyzes the text within its own context, disregarding historical aspects. Suesse-Fiedler favors the last approach, in particular the interpretation of Ruth Angress. Angress emphasized the importance of reason and tradition for the understanding of *Nathan the Wise* and held that the end of the play reconciles those contradictory concepts (Angress 1971). With her interpretation, Angress fulfilled the expectations that Lessing had of his readers, Suesse-Fiedler writes (23). She subscribes to the view that of the various ways of interpreting the play, there is only one that Lessing intended. The major part of her book is an analysis of the play itself. The questions she poses are: What does the text achieve, how does it achieve it, and what was Lessing's intention (54)? One of her conclusions is that Lessing wanted to manipulate his readers into thinking for themselves (295). Unfortunately, she adds, this intention remained undiscovered by most critics (296).

Christoph Türcke's article "Die geheime Kraft des Ringes [The Secret Power of the Ring]" (1981) asks what tolerance actually is. Certainly not, Türcke answers, the ability to accept everyone, no matter how misguided his or her thinking. Türcke regrets that *Nathan the Wise* could have ever been so misunderstood (155 and 161).[19] Modern critics, especially, should know better. Türcke accuses today's Western societies of abusing the idea of pluralism in order to achieve power. Whereas orthodox Christians were intolerant and dogmatic, modern oppressors allow everyone a measure of freedom of thought to achieve the same effect: to keep society from any serious rebellion (161). The ring parable, Türcke writes, could have taught the bourgeoisie how to question authority, but the lesson was not learned. Society eventually fell subject to pluralism and thus lost its chance at autonomy (160).

---

[19] A similar thought is expressed by Fritz Raddatz. Lessing, he says, was too much of a skeptic to break into bleating that "all men are equal" (1981, 42).

During the last couple of decades, academic life has been shaken by self-criticism. Older traditions have also become suspect. Lessing scholars, too, have begun to notice the recurring tropes and clichés that do not help in understanding Lessing but that tell much about the critics who use them. A few of the clichés persistently used in Lessing criticism in the last two hundred years depict him as the lonely fighter, the troublesome ("unbequeme") writer whose work and personality have not stopped provoking the "Establishment" (cf. Bohnen 1982, 180), and the "unpoetic" poet (cf. Steinmetz 1969, Strohschneider-Kohrs 1981). Lessing is also frequently presented as one of Germany's great men, and his name appears next to those of Luther, Goethe, and Schiller (the predominant interpretation throughout the nineteenth century), or Heine and Nietzsche (Kesten 1953, 489).

Jürgen Schröder tackled the first of these clichés in his essay "Der 'Kämpfer' Lessing [The Fighter Lessing]" (1981). He notices that the intelligentsia and the bourgeois class of nineteenth-century Germany identified with the fighter Lessing, regardless of their political or philosophical convictions (96). Schröder's own emphasis is on Lessing the pacifist (108). By transforming the historical figure into a dehistoricized stereotype, by reducing Lessing's personality and his work to one irrational aspect, critics were able to make Lessing fit their various ideological frameworks, Schröder explains (99f.). Going beyond Schröder's observations, one might add that *all* the clichés that concentrate on Lessing's character mythify him and limit the impact Lessing might have had.

Helmut Fuhrmann summarizes in his essay "Lessings *Nathan der Weise* und das Wahrheitsproblem [Lessing's *Nathan the Wise* and the Problem of Truth]" (1983) the meaning Lessing's play can have for us today. He differentiates four levels of meaning. First, the epistemological idea that belief cannot be knowledge is still valid (81). Second, *Nathan the Wise* gives us hints on how to act. It not only suggests tolerance as a philosophy, but demands that people act accordingly. Third, reason as demonstrated in the play has the power to dissolve prejudice. Fuhrmann reminds his readers that religious prejudice still exists, be it in Northern Ireland or in Iran. The Holocaust, of course, happened because of racial prejudices (83). *Nathan the Wise*, Fuhrmann seems to hope, might be used in the fight against prejudice. At this point Fuhrmann refers to Günther Anders, who has pointed to the power of metaphor. Nathan's words may touch some anti-Semites more, Anders suggested, than the report given by a modern-day Jew. Lastly, Fuhrmann concludes his essay, *Nathan the Wise* puts in doubt not only individual prejudices but ideologies — Furhmann refers to communism in particular — in their entirety (84).

In his article "Lessing und die Toleranz — Toleranzerziehung und Literaturunterricht [Lessing and Tolerance — Education to Tolerance and Literary Studies]" (1986), Jürgen Kreft emphasizes that *Nathan the Wise* can teach tolerance, but only if it is taught in a relevant way (210). It needs to be discussed as a drama that is about the past but as one that touches the student's own experience (215f.). A parallel with the current hatred of foreign workers in Germany might be successfully drawn in class discussion, Kreft suggests.

h: Where to Go from Here

Even after German unification, Lessing criticism might very well remain as diversified and contradictory as it has been throughout the last two centuries. Some of the approaches will probably make more sense than others, but in any case, what we will learn most about will be, as always, the respective author's ideological framework. This is not to say, however, that interpretation is irrelevant. The past 220 years of critical reception of *Nathan the Wise*, if it is understood in its historical context, offers an abundance of insight into the text. As a new generation and as modern readers (viewers), we have to ask the questions that make the play relevant to us.

One recent attempt to render *Nathan the Wise* significant for our time is George Taboris's adaptation of Lessing's play on the stage of the Wolfenbüttel theater in the fall of 1991 (cf. *Der Spiegel* 1991; Wille 1991). Taboris's *Nathans Tod* [Nathan's Death] takes advantage of the fact that most German viewers are at least vaguely familiar with the play. It counts on certain expectations preexisting in the audience — an important aspect of reception history that should not be overlooked by literary theory (cf. Raschdau 1979, 263) — only to break away. Nathan is confronted with a Saladin who is not interested in his parable. The Templar whose troop was responsible for the pogrom that killed Nathan's family betrays Nathan to the Patriarch. Nathan dies a broken man. Sittah, yet another victim of the senseless exercise of power, commits suicide kneeling beside Nathan's dead body. Saladin and the Patriarch are the cynical winners in the end. They are happy to be rid of the irksome Jew and make fun of the "blöde Märchen von irgendwelchen Ringen [stupid tale of some rings]" (Wille 1991, 3). Taboris's *Nathans Tod* hopes to make the audience think twice about the assumption that reason can achieve much in a corrupt and power-hungry world.

Taboris's unconventional adaptation of Lessing's play may be considered disrespectful toward its original. Yet, by straying from the classical text, and by bringing our knowledge and experience to it, we may gain new access. At the same time, Taboris's new approach is a powerful example of how offbeat, innovative, and thought-provoking interpretation can be. Lessing's work, especially, deserves continual reexamination and reinterpretation to uncover the meanings his text might have for us today.

Bibliography

Lessing's Works

Muncker, Franz, ed. 1968. *Gotthold Ephraim Lessings Sämtliche Schriften*. Ed. by Karl Lachmann. Stuttgart: Göschen'sche Verlagsbuchhandlung, 1886-1924. 3rd edition: Berlin.

Lessing, Gotthold Ephraim. 1970-1979. *Werke*. Ed. by Herbert G. Göpfert. München: Hanser. 8 volumes.

——. 1991. *Nathan the Wise, Minna von Barnhelm, and Other Plays and Writings*. Ed. by Peter Demetz. Continuum: New York. (= The German Library. Vol. 12.)

Works Cited in Chronological Order

Michaelis, Johann David. 1754. "Rezension über 'Die Juden.'" *Göttingische Anzeigen von gelehrten Sachen*. In Braun 1884, I 35-37, and Steinmetz 1969, 49-50.

Bibliothek der schönen Wissenschaften und der freyen Künste. 1761. [Review of Lessing's *Fabeln*] Leipzig. 7 (1): 32-55. In Braun 1884, I 159f.

Berlinische, privilegirte Zeitung. April 9, 1767. [Review of *Minna von Barnhelm*]. Also in Braun 1884, I 177f., and Steinmetz 1979, 63f.

[Eschenburg, Johann Joachim]. 1767. *Unterhaltungen*. 4th volume. In Braun 1884, I 190-194, and Steinmetz 1969, 61-63.

Sonnenfels, Josef Freiherr von. 1768. "Briefe über die Wienerische Schaubühne." In Steinmetz 1969, 64-65.

[Ramler, Karl Wilhelm]. March 28, 1772. [Review of *Emilia Galotti*]. *Berlinische Privilegirte Zeitung*. In Henning 1981, 169, and Steinmetz 1969, 86-88.

Wessely, Moses. 1772. "Gelehrte Sachen: Briefe über *Emilia Galotti*." *Beytrag zum Reichs-Postreuter Altona*. Altona. Quoted from Braun 1884, I 391-411.

Wieland, Christoph Martin. 1772. *Erfurtische gelehrte Zeitungen*. In Henning 1981, 188.

[Biester, Johann Erich]. 1777. [Review of *Emilia Galotti*]. "Anhang zu dem 13. bis 24. Bande der *Allgemeinen Deutschen Bibliothek*." In Braun 1884, II 89-92, and Steinmetz 1969, 107-109.

Gotter, Friedrich Wilhelm. September 24, 1778. [Letter to Friedrich Ludwig Wilhelm Mayer]. In Daunicht 1971, 466-467.

Gothaische gelehrte Zeitungen. December 29, 1779. "Wolfenbüttel." In Braun 1884, II 222f.

Herder, Johann Gottfried. May 1779. [Letter to Johann Georg Hamann]. In Dvoretzky 1971, 180.

Jacobi, Johann Georg. 1779. [Travel Journal]. In Daunicht 1971, 473-474.

Kaiserlich privilegirte Hamburgische Neue Zeitung. June 18, 1779. [Review of *Nathan the Wise*]. Hamburg. In Braun 1884, II 216f., and Steinmetz 1969, 109.

Königl. privilegirte Staats- und gelehrte Zeitung. July 27, 1779. [Review of *Nathan the Wise*]. Berlin. In Braun 1884, II 217f.

Neue Zeitungen von gelehrten Sachen. August 2, 1779. "Berlin." Leipzig. In Braun 1884, II 218f.

Neuer Gelehrter Mercurius. May 20, 1779. [Review of *Nathan the Wise*]. Altona. 7th volume, 156f. In Braun 1884, III 88f.

Neueste Critische Nachrichten. June 12, 1779. [Review of *Nathan the Wise*]. Greifswald. In Braun 1884, II 215f.

Nürnbergische gelehrte Zeitung. May 25, 1779. [Review of *Nathan the Wise*]. Nuremberg. Quoted from Braun 1884, II 210-214.

Staats- und Gelehrte Zeitung des Hamburgischen unpartheyischen Correspondenten. May 21, 1779. [Review of *Nathan the Wise*]. Hamburg. In Braun 1884, II 208.

Tralles, Balthasar Ludewig. 1779. *Zufällige alt-deutsche und christliche Betrachtungen über Hrn. Gotthold Ephraim Lessings Gedicht Nathan der Weise*. Breslau: Korn. 2 volumes.

Auserlesene Bibliothek der neuesten deutschen Litteratur. 1780. [Review of *Nathan the Wise*]. eighteenth volume. 391-402. Lemgo. Quoted from Braun 1884, II 346-348.

Beytrag zum Reichs-Post-Reuter. February 17, 1780. [no title]. Altona. In Braun 1884, II 254.

Der teutsche Merkur. June 1780. "Fortsetzung der Bilanz der schönen Literatur im Jahre 1779." Weimar. In Braun 1884, II 262f.

Jacobi, Friedrich Heinrich. October 24, 1780. [Letter to Johann Jakob Wilhelm Heinse.] In Dvoretzky 1971, 75 and 160.

Kielisches Litteratur-Journal. January 1780. [Review of *Nathan the Wise*]. Altona 1: 31-38. Quoted from Braun 1884, II 246-253. Also in Steinmetz 1969, 110-114.

Litteratur- und Theater-Zeitung. March 4, 1780. "Noch nähere Berichtigung des Mährchens von 1000 Dukaten oder Judas Ischarioth." Berlin. In Braun 1884, II 254-256.

[Schütz, Christian Gottfried.] 1780f. "Briefe an Madame B.**: Über Lessings Nathan den Weisen." *Litteratur- und Theater-Zeitung.* Berlin. Quoted from Braun 1884, II. 282-340.

Dohm, Christian Wilhelm. 1781. *Über die bürgerliche Verbesserung der Juden.* Berlin and Stettin: Nicolai.

Herder, Johann Gottfried. October 1781. "Gotthold Ephraim Lessing: Gebohren 1729, gestorben 1781." *Der teutsche Merkur* 3-29. Quoted from Steinmetz 1969, 123-134. Also in Braun 1884, II 397-415.

Königlich privilegirte Berlinische Zeitung von Staats- und gelehrten Sachen. May 18, 1781. [no title]. Berlin. In Braun 1884, II 393.

Küttner, Karl August. 1781. *Charaktere teutscher Dichter und Prosaisten: Von Karl, dem Großen, bis aufs Jahr 1780.* Berlin. In Steinmetz 1969, 134-135.

Mendelssohn, Moses. February 1781. [Letter to Karl Gotthelf Lessing]. In Steinmetz 1969, 122f.

Allgemeine deutsche Bibliothek. [1782? Review of *Nathan the Wise*, works by Tralles, Schütz, and Pfranger]. Berlin and Stettin. [Appendix to the 37th volume to 52nd volume, pp. 1713-1725.] Quoted from Braun 1884, III 108-118.

Der Kirchenbote für Religionsfreunde aller Kirchen. 1782. "Auszüge einiger sehr zuverläßigen Briefe aus Br. über Lessings Tod." Dessau and Leipzig 5: 576-581. Quoted from Daunicht 1971, 557-560.

Pfranger, Johann Georg. 1782. *Der Mönch vom Libanon: Ein Nachtrag zu Nathan der Weise.* Dessau: Buchhandlung der Gelehrten. Partial reprint in Stümcke 1904, 1-36.

Jacobi, Friedrich Heinrich. November 4, 1783. [Letter to Moses Mendelssohn]. Düsseldorf. Quoted from Daunicht 1971, 498-513.

Lotich, Karl. 1783. *Wer war wohl mehr Jude.* Leipzig.

Reinicke, H. 1784. *Nathan der deutsche, oder Neider sind wahre Verschnittene.* Leipzig: Schönfeldische Buchhandlung. Quoted from Stümcke 1904, 37-83.

Mendelssohn, Moses. 1785. "Morgenstunden, oder Vorlesungen über das Dasein Gottes." Quoted from Steinmetz 1969, 142-145.

Sternberg, Carl. 1787. *Menschen und Menschen-Situationen oder die Familie Grunau.* Frankfurt am Main and Leipzig.

Hottinger, Johann Jakob. 1789. *Versuch einer Vergleichung der deutschen Dichter mit den Griechen und Römern: Eine von der Kurfürstlichen deutschen Gesellschaft in Mannheim gekrönte Preisschrift.* Mannheim. Quoted from Steinmetz 1969, 153-157.

Meister, Leonard. 1789. *Charakteristik deutscher Dichter: Nach der Zeitordnung gereiht, mit Bildnissen von Heinrich Pfenninger.* St. Gallen and Leipzig: Huber und Compagnie. 2 volumes. Partial reprint in Steinmetz 1969, 151-153.

Großmann, Gustav Friedrich Wilhelm. 1791. "Lessings Denkmal: Eine vaterländische Geschichte." Hannover. Quoted from Steinmetz 1969, 157-159.

Schlegel, Friedrich. 1792. [Letter to A.W. Schlegel]. February 11, 1792. In Dvoretzky 1971, 147.

Lessing, Karl Gotthelf. 1793 - 1795. *Gotthold Ephraim Lessings Leben, nebst seinem noch übrigen litterarischen Nachlasse.* Berlin: Vossische Buchhandlung. 3 volumes.

Mendelssohn, Moses. 1795. "Hauptzüge von Lessings Persönlichkeit." In K. Lessing 1793 - 1795, II 14-19. Also in Steinmetz 1969, 167-168.

Schiller, Friedrich. 1795. "Über naive und sentimentalische Dichtung." Quoted from *Schillers Werke: Nationalausgabe.* Vol. 20. *Philosophische Schriften: Erster Teil.* Ed. by Benno von Wiese. 1962. Weimar: Hermann Böhlaus Nachfolger. 413-503.

Schlegel, Friedrich. 1797. "Über Lessing." *Lyceum der schönen Künste.* Quoted from Steinmetz 1969, 169-188.

Herder, Johann Gottfried. 1801. *Adrastrea.* Quoted from Dvoretzky 1971, 118-119.

Schiller, Friedrich. 1801. *Nathan der Weise* [revised for the stage]. Quoted from *Schillers Werke. Nationalausgabe.* Vol. 13. *Bühnenbearbeitungen. Erster Teil.* Ed. by Hans Heinrich Borcherdt. 1949. Weimar: Hermann Böhlaus Nachfolger.

Schlegel, Friedrich. 1801. [Continuation of "Über Lessing"]. *Charakteristiken und Kritiken*. Königsberg. Quoted from Steinmetz 1969, 188-195.

Herder, Johann Gottfried. 1802. "Bekehrung der Juden." Quoted from *Sämmtliche Werke*. Ed. by Bernhard Suphan. 1886 Berlin: Weidmannsche Buchhandlung. Vol. 24. 61-67.

Jean Paul. 1804. *Vorschule der Ästhetik*. Quoted from Steinmetz 1969, 260-261.

Schlegel, Friedrich. 1804. "Lessings Gedanken und Meinungen." Quoted from Behler 1975 [therein "Vom Charakter der Protestanten"]. 46-102.

Voss, Julius von. 1804. *Der travestirte Nathan der Weise. Posse in zwey Akten, mit Intermezzos, Choren, Tanz, gelehrtem Zweykampf, Mord und Todschlag*. Berlin: Johann Wilhelm Schmidt. Reprinted 1985. Bern and New York: Peter Lang. (= Seltene Texte aus der deutschen Romantik, vol. 2). Quoted from Stümcke 1804, 131-218.

Engel, Johann Jakob. 1806. *Schriften*. Vol. 11. Berlin: Myliussische Buchhandlung. [The *Poetik* first appeared in 1783. A facsimile edition of The *Schriften* appeared in 1971, Frankfurt am Main: Athenäum.]

Müller, Adam. 1806. *Vorlesungen über die deutsche Wissenschaft und Literatur*. Quoted from Steinmetz 1969, 226.

Goethe, Johann Wolfgang von. 1811-1814. *Dichtung und Wahrheit: Aus meinem Leben*. Quoted from Steinmetz 1969, 231-233. Partial reprint also in Dvoretzky 1971, 165-168.

Bouterwek, Friedrich. 1819. *Geschichte der Poesie und Beredsamkeit seit dem Ende des dreizehnten Jahrhunderts*. Göttingen. Quoted from Steinmetz 1969, 240-241.

Tieck, Ludwig. 1825. *Das deutsche Drama*. Quoted from Dvoretzky 1971, 231-232.

Heine, Heinrich. 1835. *Zur Geschichte der Religion und Philosophie in Deutschland*. Quoted from Steinmetz 1969, 262-266.

—— 1836. *Die romantische Schule*. Quoted from Steinmetz 1969, 260-261.

Menzel, Wolfgang. [2]1836. *Die deutsche Literatur*. Stuttgart. Quoted from Steinmetz 1969, 276-281.

Rießer, Gabriel. 1838. "Über Lessing: An die Israeliten Deutschlands." Quoted from Deutsch-Israelischer Gemeindebund. 1879, 255-282.

Laube, Heinrich. 1839. *Geschichte der deutschen Literatur*. Stuttgart: Kallberger'sche Verlagsbuchhandlung. 2 volumes.

Hebbel, Friedrich. December 30, 1841. [Diary]. Quoted from Steinmetz 1969, 289.

Gervinus, Georg Gottfried. 1840. *Neuere Geschichte der poetischen National-Literatur der Deutschen: Von Gottsched's Zeiten bis zu Göthe's Jugend.* Leipzig: Wilhelm Engelmann. Quoted from the second edition, 1843.

Vischer, Friedrich Theodor. 1846-1857. *Ästhetik oder Wissenschaft des Schönen.* Quoted from Robert Vischer. 1923. *Zum Gebrauche für Vorlesungen von Friedrich Theodor Vischer.* Munich: Meyer & Jesse. 2nd edition.

Ruge, Arnold. 1847. *Sämmtliche Werke.* Vol. 1. *Geschichte der deutschen Poesie und Philosophie seit Lessing.* Mannheim: Grohe.

Danzel, Theodor W. and G.E. Guhrauer. 1850 - 1854. *Gotthold Ephraim Lessing, sein Leben und seine Werke.* 2 volumes. Leipzig: Verlag der Dyk'schen Buchhandlung.

Eichendorff, Joseph von. 1851. *Der deutsche Roman des achtzehnten Jahrhunderts in seinem Verhältniß zum Christenthum.* Leipzig: Brockhaus. Quoted from Mauser 1965, VIII/2: 1-245.

——. 1854. *Zur Geschichte des Dramas.* Leipzig: Brockhaus. Quoted from Mauser 1965, VIII/2: 247-424.

Ludwig, Otto. [1855-1865?]. *Dramatische Studien.* Berlin, Leipzig, Stuttgart, and Vienna: Bong. Quoted from Dvoretzky 1971, II 339-348.

Tieck, Ludwig. 1855. *Erinnerungen aus dem Leben des Dichters nach dessen mündlichen und schriftlichen Mittheilungen.* Ed. by Rudolf Köpke. Leipzig. Quoted from Steinmetz 1969, 312-314.

Köpke, Ernst. 1856. "Über 'Nathan den Weisen.'" *Zeitschrift für das Gymnasialwesen.* Quoted from Steinmetz 1969, 337-339.

Eichendorff, Joseph von. 1857. *Geschichte der poetischen Literatur Deutschlands.* Paderborn: Schöningh. Quoted from Mauser 1965, IX 3-492.

Stahr, Adolf. 1859. *Lessing: Sein Leben und seine Werke.* Berlin 1859. Quoted from Steinmetz 1969, 339-344.

Goldschmidt, Abraham Meyer. 1860. "Zweite Rede bei der Lessing-Feier in Leipzig." *Die erste Lessing-Feier in Leipzig.* Leipzig: Schillerverein. Quoted from Steinmetz 1969, 346-348.

Lassalle, Ferdinand. 1861. "Gotthold Ephraim Lessing." Hamburg. Quoted from *Gesammelte Reden und Schriften.* Ed. by Eduard Bernstein. Vol. 6, *Philosophisch-literarische Streifzüge.* 1919. Berlin: Cassirer. 153-188.

Strauß, David Friedrich. 1861. "Über Lessing's 'Nathan': Ein Vortrag." Quoted from Bohnen 1984, 11-45. Also in Steinmetz 1969, 363-366.

Geiger, Abraham. 1862. "Zum Lessing-Denkmal: Ein Aufruf, namentlich an die Juden." *Jüdische Zeitschrift für Wissenschaft und Leben.* Breslau. 85. Quoted from Deutsch-Israelischer Gemeindebund 1879, 283-287.

Hebler, C. 1862. *Lessing-Studien.* Bern: Huber und Comp.

Treitschke, Heinrich von. 1863. "Lessing." *Grenzbote.* Quoted from Steinmetz 1969, 373-380.

Köpke, Ernst. 1865. "Studien zu Lessings Nathan." *Ritter-Akademie zu Brandenburg.* Vol. 9. Brandenburg: Müller. 3-39.

Dilthey, Wilhelm. 1867. "Die Weltanschauung Lessings." Quoted from *Das Erlebnis und die Dichtung: Lessing. Goethe. Novalis. Hölderlin.* 1906. Leipzig: Teubner. Also in Bohnen 1984, 11-45, and Steinmetz 1969, 423-434.

Scherer, Wilhelm. 1870. "Zu Lessings 'Nathan.'" Quoted from his *Vorträge und Aufsätze zur Geschichte des geistigen Lebens in Deutschland und Österreich.* 1874. Berlin: Weidmannsche Buchhandlung, 328-336.

Auerbach, Berthold. 1879. "Gedanken über Lessing's 'Nathan.'" In Deutsch-Israelischer Gemeindebund 1879, 321-328.

Bodek, Arnold. 1879. "Warum ist Nathan ein Jude? Stimmen aus der Lessing Literatur." In Deutsch-Israelischer Gemeindebund 1879, 350-376.

Deutsch-Israelischer Gemeindebund, ed. 1879. *Lessing-Mendelssohn-Gedenkbuch. Zur hundertfünfzigjährigen Geburtsfeier von Gotthold Ephraim Lessing und Moses Mendelssohn, sowie zur Säcularfeier von Lessing's "Nathan."* Leipzig: Baumgärtner's Buchhandlung.

Marr, Wilhelm. [7]1879. *Der Sieg des Judenthums über das Germanenthum: Vom nicht confessionellen Standpunkt aus betrachtet.* Bern: Costenoble.

Wünsche, Aug. 1879. "Der Ursprung der Parabel von den drei Ringen." *Grenzbote* 4. In Deutsch-Israelischer Gemeindebund 1879, 329-349.

Maltzahn, W. von and R. Boxberger, eds. 1880 - 1881. *Gotthold Ephraim Lessing: Sein Leben und seine Werke,* by Theodor W. Danzel and G.E. Guhrauer. Berlin: Hofmann. 2 volumes.

Mayr, Richard. 1880. *Beiträge zur Beurtheilung G.E. Lessing's.* Vienna: Alfred Hölder.

Auerbach, Berthold. January 22, 1881. [Letter to Jakob Auerbach]. Quoted from Dvoretzky 1971, II 379.

Auerbach, Ludwig. 1881. *Die Genesis des Nathan: Gedenkworte zu Lessing's hundertjährigem Todestag.* Berlin. Quoted from Steinmetz 1969, 389-390.

Fischer, Kuno. [3]1881. *G. E. Lessing als Reformator der deutschen Literatur.* 2 volumes. Stuttgart: Cotta.

Scherer, Wilhelm. 1881. "Gotthold Ephraim Lessing: Zum 15. Februar 1881." *Deutsche Rundschau* 26: 272-299. Quoted from Bohnen 1982, 58-70.

Schmidt, Julian. 1881. "Lessing: 15. Februar 1881." Quoted from Bohnen 1982, 71-88.

Braun, Julius. 1884, 1893, and 1897. *Lessing im Urtheile seiner Zeitgenossen: Zeitungskritiken, Berichte und Notizen, Lessing und seine Werke betreffend, aus den Jahren 1747-1781.* Berlin: Friedrich Stahn. 3 volumes.

Schmidt, Erich. 1884 - 1886. *Lessing: Geschichte seines Lebens und seiner Schriften.* Berlin: Weidmannsche Buchhandlung. 2 volumes. Second edition 1899, third edition 1909. Partial reprint in Steinmetz 1969, 396-399.

Mauthner, Fritz. 1886. "Um Lessing." In his *Credo: Gesammelte Aufsätze.* Berlin: J.J. Heine. 188-193. Quoted from Steinmetz 1969, 399-402.

Brunner, Sebastian. 1890. *Lessingiasis und Nathanolgie: Eine Religionsstörung im Lessing- und Nathan-Cultus.* Paderborn.

Mehring, Franz. 1893. *Die Lessing-Legende.* Stuttgart: Dietz. Quoted from his *Gesammelte Schriften.* Ed. Thomas Höhle, Hans Koch, and Josef Schleifstein. Vol. 9. 1983. Berlin: Dietz.

Gast, E.R. 1898. "Bemerkungen zu einigen Schulausgaben von Lessings Nathan dem Weisen." *Zeitschrift für den deutschen Unterricht* 12: 778-788.

Stümcke, Heinrich, ed. 1904. *Die Fortsetzungen, Nachahmungen und Travestien von Lessings "Nathan der Weise."* Berlin: Selbstverlag der Gesellschaft für Theatergeschichte.

Dühring, Eugen. [2]1906. *Die Überschätzung Lessing's und seiner Befassung mit Literatur: Zugleich eine neue kritische Dramentheorie.* Leipzig: Verlag von Theod. Thomas.

Lienhard, Friedrich. 1907. *Wege nach Weimar: Beiträge zur Erneuerung des Idealismus.* Quoted from Steinmetz 1969, 419-420.

Mehring, Franz. 1909. "Nathan der Weise." Quoted from his *Gesammelte Schriften*. Ed. by. Thomas Höhle, Hans Koch, and Josef Schleifstein. Vol. 9. 1983. Berlin: Dietz, 418-423.

Krüger, Johanna. 1913. *Friedrich Schlegels Bekehrung zu Lessing*. Weimar: Duncker. (= Forschungen zur neueren Literaturgeschichte). Quoted from the reprinted edition 1978. Hildesheim: Gerstenberg.

Nadler, Josef. 1913. *Literaturgeschichte der deutschen Stämme und Landschaften*. Regensburg: Habbel.

Kappstein, Theodor. 1915. "Der kriegerische Lessing. Ein Vortrag." *Lessing-Museum*. Berlin. Quoted from Steinmetz 1969, 440-443.

Bartels, Adolf. 1918. *Lessing und die Juden*. Dresden: C.A. Koch.

Fittbogen, Gottfried. 1923. *Die Religion Lessings*. Leipzig: Mayer & Müller. 148-182. Quoted from Bohnen 1984, 62-93.

Brüggemann, Fritz. 1925. "Die Weisheit in Lessings 'Nathan.'" *Zeitschrift für Deutschkunde* 39: 557-582. Quoted from Bauer 1968, 74-82.

Borchardt, Rudolf. 1929. "Lessing. Rückblick auf ein Jubiläumsjahr." *Deutsche Allgemeine Zeitung* 68. Quoted from Steinmetz 1969, 454-463.

Cassirer, Ernst. 1929. "Die Idee der Religion bei Lessing und Mendelssohn." *Festgabe zum zehnjährigen Bestehen der Akademie für die Wissenschaft des Judentums: 1919-29*. Berlin. 22-41. Quoted from Bohnen 1984, 94-115.

Heuss, Theodor. 1929. "Gotthold Ephraim Lessing." *Monatshefte für die Deutschen im Ausland*. Quoted from Steinmetz 1969, 443-447.

Hofmannsthal, Hugo von. 1929. "Gotthold Ephraim Lessing: Zum 22. Januar 1929." *Neue Freie Presse*. Quoted from Steinmetz 1969, 451-454.

Mann, Thomas. 1929a. "Zu Lessings Gedächtnis." *Berliner Tageblatt*. Quoted from Steinmetz 1969, 448-451.

——. 1929b. "Rede über Lessing." *Preußische Akademie der Künste: Jahrbuch der Sektion für Dichtkunst*. 150-160. Quoted from Bauer 1968, 127-142.

Richter, Julius. 1930. "Rückblick aufs Lessingjahr 1929." *Zeitschrift für Deutschkunde* 44 (9): 562-576.

Leisegang, Hans. 1931. "Nathan der Weise." In his *Lessings Weltanschauung*. Leipzig: Felix Meiner, 140-158. Quoted from Bohnen 1984, 116-132.

Mann, Heinrich. 1931. "Lessing." [Lecture given on the Berlin Radio on February 15, 1931]. In his *Essays*. Vol. I. 1954. Berlin: Aufbau, 450-458.

Wiese, Benno von. 1931. "Nathan der Weise." In his *Lessing. Dichtung, Aesthetik, Philosophie*. Leipzig: Quelle und Meyer, 64-85. Quoted from Bohnen 1984, 133-152.

Nadler, Josef. [3]1932. *Literaturgeschichte der deutschen Stämme und Landschaften*. 4 volumes. Regensburg: Josef Habbel.

Wiese, Benno von. 1932. "Humanität bei Lessing." *Germanisch-Romanische Monatsschrift* 20: 324-326. Quoted from Bauer 1968, 172-175.

Adams, Paul. 1933. ["Shakespeare – ein Kriterium für nationale Zuverlässigkeit."] *Deutsches Volkstum*. 945-949. Quoted from Wulf 1989, 152f.

Herzfelde, Wieland. 1933. "Wir sollen deutsch reden." *Neue deutsche Blätter* 1 (1): 2-3. Quoted from Matthias Wegner. *Exil und Literatur: Deutsche Schriftsteller im Ausland: 1933-1945*. [2]1968. Frankfurt am Main: Athenäum.

Bartels, Adolf. [2]1934. *Lessing und die Juden: Eine Untersuchung*. Leipzig: Theodor Weicher.

Burger, Heinz Otto. 1934. "Die rassischen Kräfte im deutschen Schrifttum." *Zeitschrift für Deutschkunde* 48: 462-476.

Fricke, Gerhard. 1934. "Das Humanitätsideal der klassischen deutschen Dichtung und die deutsche Gegenwart: I. Lessing." *Zeitschrift für Deutschkunde* 48: 273-292.

Fechner, Hellmut. 1935. "Gedankentiefe." *Nationalsozialistische Erziehung*. 321. Quoted from Wulf 1989, 400f.

Fritsch, Theodor. [38]1935. *Handbuch der Judenfrage: Die wichtigsten Tatsachen zur Beurteilung des jüdischen Volkes*. Leipzig: Hammer Verlag.

Mann, Otto. 1935. "Neue Lessingforschung." *Zeitschrift für deutsche Philologie* 59: 374-380.

Die Rote Fahne. 1936. "Lessings Antwort an Göbbels." 5: 5.

Labus, Lotte. [1936?]. "'Minna von Barnhelm' auf der deutschen Bühne." Diss. Friedr. Wilhelm Universität zu Berlin.

Poethen, Wilhelm. 1936. "Die Lesestoffauswahl im Rahmen der heutigen Forderungen." *Zeitschrift für deutsche Bildung* 12: 14-27.

Thielicke, Helmut. 1936. *Vernunft und Offenbarung*. Gütersloh: Bertelsmann.

Langenbucher, Hellmuth. 1937. *Deutsche Dichtung in Vergangenheit und Gegenwart: Eine Einführung mit ausgewählten Textproben*. Berlin: Verlagshaus Bong.

Linden, Walther. 1937. *Geschichte der deutschen Literatur von den Anfängen bis zur Gegenwart*. Leipzig: Reclam. Quoted from the fourth edition 1942.

Ludendorff, Mathilde. 1937. *Lessings Geisteskampf und Lebensschicksal*. München: Ludendorffs Verlag GmbH.

Simon, H.O. 1937. "Für Wahrheit, Freiheit und Menschlichkeit." *Das Wort* 2 (3): 53-56.

Wundt, Max. 1937. "Nathan der Weise oder Aufklärung und Judentum." In Sitzungsbericht der ersten Arbeitstagung der Forschungsabteilung Judenfrage des Reichsinstitut für Geschichte des neuen Deutschlands. 1937. *Forschungen zur Judenfrage*. Hamburg: Hanseatische Verlagsanstalt. Vol. 1. 136-140.

Nadler, Josef. [4]1938. *Literaturgeschichte des Deutschen Volkes: Dichtung und Schrifttum der deutschen Stämme und Landschaften*. 4 volumes. Berlin: Propyläen-Verlag.

Suter, Ernst. 1938. "Lessing politisch gesehen." *Zeitschrift für Deutschkunde* 52: 414-420.

Bach, Rudolf. 1940. *Der Aufbruch des deutschen Geistes: Lessing — Klopstock — Herder*. Markleeberg bei Leipzig: Karl Rauch.

Frenzel, Elisabeth. 1940. *Judengestalten auf der deutschen Bühne: Ein notwendiger Querschnitt durch 700 Jahre Rollengeschichte*. Munich: Deutscher Volksverlag. (Second edition 1942).

Jancke, Oskar. 1940. "Über die Prosa Lessings." *Die Literatur* 42: 328-331.

Zimmermann, Werner. 1940. "Die Gestalt des Juden in der deutschen Dichtung der Aufklärungszeit: Ein Beitrag zur Geschichte der Emanzipation des Judentums." *Zeitschrift für Deutschkunde* 54: 245-253.

Fechter, Paul. [4]1941. *Geschichte der deutschen Literatur: Von den Anfängen bis zur Gegenwart*. Berlin: Th. Knaur Nachfolger.

Lenz, Harold. 1941. "Der Deutschlehrer und Lessings' Nathan." *German Quarterly* 14: 121-127 and 170-175. Quoted from Bohnen 1984, 405-418.

Wiese, Benno von. 1941. "Die deutsche Leistung der Aufklärung." In Gerhard Fricke, Franz Koch and Klemens Lugowski, eds. *Von deutscher Art in Sprache und Dichtung*. Stuttgart und Berlin: Kohlhammer. Vol. III, 241-269.

Bab, Julius. 1944. "Lessing." *Deutsche Blätter* 2 (7): 262-265.

Horkheimer, Max and Theodor W. Adorno. 1947. *Dialektik der Aufklärung: Philosophische Fragmente.* New edition 1971. Frankfurt am Main: Fischer.

Thielicke, Helmut. 1947. *Vernunft und Offenbarung.* Gütersloh: Bertelsmann.

Mann, Otto. 1948. *Lessing: Sein und Leistung.* Hamburg: Marion von Schröder Verlag.

Berendsohn, Walter A. 1949. *Die humanistische Front: Einführung in die deutsche Emigranten-Literatur.* Vol. II. *Vom Kriegsausbruch 1939 bis Ende 1946.* Quoted from the reprinted edition 1976. Worms: Georg Heintz.

Hazard, Paul. 1949. *Die Herrschaft der Vernunft: Das europäische Denken im 18. Jahrhundert.* Hamburg: Hoffmann und Campe.

Nigg, Walter. 1949. *Das Buch der Ketzer.* Zurich: Artemis.

Atkins, Stuart. 1951. "The Parable of the Rings in Lessing's 'Nathan der Weise.'" *Germanic Review* 26 (1): 259-267. Quoted from Bohnen 1984, 155-167.

Barth, Karl. 1952. *Die protestantische Theologie im 19. Jahrhundert.* Zurich: Evangelischer Verlag. Quoted from his *Protestant Thought: From Rousseau to Ritschl.* 1971. Freeport, New York: Books for Libraries Press.

Rasch, Wolfdietrich. 1952. "Die Zeit der Klassik und frühen Romantik." In *Annalen der deutschen Literatur: Geschichte der deutschen Literatur von den Anfängen bis zur Gegenwart. Eine Gemeinschaftsarbeit zahlreicher Fachgelehrter.* Ed. by Heinz Otto Burger. Stuttgart: Metzler. 465-550.

Kesten, Hermann. 1953. "Was bleibt." Quoted from Dvoretzky 1971, II 489.

Mayer, Hans. 1953. "Lessing, Mitwelt und Nachwelt." In his *Studien zur deutschen Literaturgeschichte.* Berlin. 39-61. Quoted from Bauer 1968, 260-286.

Schneider, Johannes. 1953. "Lessings Stellung zur Theologie." In his *Lessings Stellung zur Theologie vor der Herausgabe der Wolfenbüttler Fragmente.* The Hague: Excelsior. Quoted from Bauer 1968, 287-301.

Bizet, J. A. 1955. "La Sagesse de Nathan". *Etudes Germaniques* 10: 269-275. Quoted from Bauer 1968, 302-311.

Ziegler, Klaus. 1955. "Das deutsche Drama der Neuzeit." In Wolfgang Stammler, ed. *Deutsche Philologie im Aufriß.* 1955-1956. II 1997-2350. Berlin: Erich Schmidt. Quoted from the second edition, 1960.

Mann, Otto. 1956. "Lessing und die moderne Wissenschaft." *Der Deutschunterricht* 8 (5): 68-86. Quoted from Bauer 1968, 312-335.

Rasch, Wolfdietrich. 1956. "Die Literatur der Aufklärungszeit: Ein Forschungsbericht." *Deutsche Vierteljahrsschrift für Literaturwissenschaft und Geistesgeschichte* 30 (4): 533-560.

Chiarini, Paolo. 1957. "Lessing und Brecht: Einiges über die Beziehung von Epik und Dramatik." *Sinn und Form: Beiträge zur Literatur. 2. Sonderheft. Bertolt Brecht.* 188-203.

Thielicke, Helmut. [3]1957. *Offenbarung, Vernunft und Existenz.* Gütersloh: Bertelsmann. (First and second editions as *Vernunft und Offenbarung.* 1936 and 1947).

Politzer, Heinz. 1958. "Lessings Parabel von den drei Ringen." *German Quarterly* 31: 161-177. Quoted from Bauer 1968, 343-361.

Rohrmoser, Günter. 1958. "Lessing. Nathan der Weise." In *Das deutsche Drama. Vom Barock bis zur Gegenwart.* Ed. by Benno von Wiese. Düsseldorf: August Bagel. 113-126.

Arendt, Hannah. 1960. *Von der Menschlichkeit in finsteren Zeiten: Rede über Lessing.* Munich: Piper. Quoted from Steinmetz 1969, 486-494.

Kesten, Hermann. 1960. "Gotthold Ephraim Lessing: Ein deutscher Moralist." *Akademie der Wissenschaften und Literatur: Abhandlungen der Klasse der Literatur.* Quoted from Steinmetz 1969, 478-486.

Maurer, Warren R. 1962. "The Integration of the Ring Parable in Lessing's 'Nathan der Weise.'" *Monatshefte für deutschen Unterricht, deutsche Sprache und Literatur* 54 (2): 49-57.

Cases, Cesare. 1963. "Lessings 'Nathan der Weise.'" *Saggi e note di letterature tedesca.* Turin. Quoted from Bohnen 1984, 331-340.

Dvoretzky, Edward. 1963. *The Enigma of Emilia Galotti.* The Hague: Nijhoff.

Kesten, Hermann. 1963. "Gotthold Ephraim Lessing: Ein Moralist in Deutschland." Quoted from Dvoretzky 1971, II 491-503.

Herrlitz, Hans-Georg. 1964. *Der Lektüre-Kanon des Deutschunterrichts im Gymnasium: Ein Beitrag zur Geschichte der muttersprachlichen Schulliteratur.* Heidelberg: Quelle & Meyer.

Plavius, Heinz. 1964. "Revision des Humanismus: Die Wandlungen im Lessing-Bild der westdeutschen Reaktion." *Neue deutsche Literatur* 12 (9): 94-109.

Boehlich, Walter, ed. 1965. *Der Berliner Antisemitismusstreit.* Frankfurt am Main: Insel.

Mauser, Wolfram, ed. 1965ff. *Literarhistorische Schriften von Freiherrn Joseph von Eichendorff.* Regensburg: Hebbel.

Schrimpf, Hans Joachim. 1965. *Lessing und Brecht: Von der Aufklärung auf dem Theater.* Pfullingen: Neske.

Ziegler, Klaus. 1965. "Deutsche Sprach- und Literaturwissenschaft im Dritten Reich." In Flitner, Andreas, ed. *Deutsches Geistesleben und Nationalsozialismus.* Tübingen: Rainer Wunderlich.

Demetz, Peter. 1966. *Gotthold Ephraim Lessing: Nathan der Weise.* Frankfurt am Main and Berlin: Ullstein.

Heller, Peter. 1966. *Dialectics and Nihilism: Essays on Lessing, Nietzsche, Mann and Kafka.* Amherst: University of Massachusetts Press. Quoted from Bohnen 1984, 219-228.

Conrady, Karl Otto. 1967. "Deutsche Literaturwissenschaft und Drittes Reich." In Eberhard Lämmert *et al.*, eds. *Germanistik — eine deutsche Wissenschaft.* Frankfurt am Main: Suhrkamp, 71-109.

Lämmert, Eberhard. 1967. "Germanistik — eine deutsche Wissenschaft." In Lämmert *et al.*, eds. *Germanistik — eine deutsche Wissenschaft.* Frankfurt am Main: Suhrkamp, 7-41.

Bauer, Gerhard and Sibylle Bauer. 1968. *Gotthold Ephraim Lessing.* Darmstadt: Wissenschaftliche Buchgesellschaft. (= Wege der Forschung. Vol. 211).

Hodge, James L. 1968. "Men, Moods, and Modals in Nathan der Weise." In *Helen Adolf Festschrift.* Ed. by Scheema Z. Buene, J. L. Hodge, Luc B. Pinto. New York: Ungar, 166-186.

Emircan, Belma. 1969. "Homo Humanus. Betrachtungen zu Lessings Nathan." In Götz Grossklaus, ed. *Geistesgeschichtliche Perspektiven: Rückblick — Augenblick — Ausblick.* Bonn: Bouvier, 213-226.

Guthke, Karl S. 1969. "Lessing-Literatur 1963-1968." *Lessing Yearbook* 1: 255-264.

Steinmetz, Horst. 1969. *Lessing — ein unpoetischer Dichter: Dokumente aus drei Jahrhunderten zur Wirkungsgeschichte Lessings in Deutschland.* Frankfurt am Main and Bonn: Athenäum.

Talbert, Charles H., ed. 1970. *Reimarus: Fragments.* Transl. by Ralph S. Fraser. Philadelphia: Fortress.

Angress, Ruth K. 1971. "Dreams That Were More than Dreams in Lessing's *Nathan der Weise.*" *Lessing Yearbook* 3: 108-127.

Böhler, Michael J. 1971. "Lessings *Nathan der Weise* als Spiel vom Grunde." *Lessing Yearbook* 3: 128-150.

Brown, F. Andrew. 1971. *Gotthold Ephraim Lessing.* New York: Twayne.

Daunicht, Richard. 1971. *Lessing im Gespräch: Berichte und Urteile von Freunden und Zeitgenossen.* Munich: Fink.

Demetz, Peter. 1971. "Die Folgenlosigkeit Lessings." *Merkur: Deutsche Zeitschrift für europäisches Denken* 25 (8): 726-741.

Dvoretzky, Edward, ed. 1971 - 1972. *Lessing: Dokumente zur Wirkungsgeschichte 1755-1968.* 2 volumes. Göppingen: Verlag Alfred Kümmerle.

Göbel, Helmut. 1971. "Die Bildlichkeit im 'Nathan.'" In his *Bild und Sprache bei Lessing.* Munich: Fink, 154-195. Quoted from Bohnen 1984, 229-266.

Hernadi, Paul. 1971. "Nathan der Bürger: Lessings Mythos vom aufgeklärten Kaufmann." *Lessing Yearbook* 3: 151-159. Quoted from Bohnen 1984, 341-349.

Liepert, Anita. 1971. "Lessing-Bilder: Zur Metamorphose der bürgerlichen Lessingforschung." *Deutsche Zeitschrift für Philosophie* 19: 1318-1330.

Lützeler, Paul Michael. 1971. "Die marxistische Lessing-Rezeption: Darstellung und Kritik am Beispiel von Mehring und Lukács." *Lessing Yearbook* 3: 173-193.

Mann, Heinrich. 1971. *Verteidigung der Kultur: Antifaschistische Streitschriften und Essays.* Ed. by Werner Herden. Berlin: Aufbau.

Pelters, Wilm. 1972. *Lessings Standort: Sinndeutung der Geschichte als Kern seines Denkens.* Heidelberg: Stiehm.

Schröder, Jürgen. 1972. "'Nathan der Weise': Ein Drama der Verständigung." In his *Gotthold Ephraim Lessing: Sprache und Drama.* Munich: Fink, 247-268.

Altmann, Alexander. 1973. *Moses Mendelssohn: A biographical Study.* Alabama: University of Alabama Press.

Frank, Horst Joachim. 1973. *Geschichte des Deutschunterrichts: Von den Anfängen bis 1945.* Munich: Hanser.

Mayer, Hans. 1973. "Der weise Nathan und der Räuber Spiegelberg: Antinomien der jüdischen Emanzipation in Deutschland." *Jahrbuch der Deutschen Schillergesellschaft* 17: 253-272. Quoted from Bohnen 1984, 350-373.

Rilla, Paul. 1973. *Lessing und sein Zeitalter*. Munich: C.H. Beck. [First edition, 1958. Berlin and Weimar: Aufbau.]

Schlaffer, Heinz. 1973. *Der Bürger als Held: Sozialgeschichtliche Auflösungen literarischer Widersprüche*. Frankfurt am Main: Suhrkamp.

Seeba, Hinrich C. 1973. *Die Liebe zur Sache: Öffentliches und privates Interesse in Lessings Dramen*. Tübingen: Max Niemeyer. (= Untersuchungen zur deutschen Literaturgeschichte. Vol. 9).

Seifert, Siegfried. 1973. *Lessing-Bibliographie*. Berlin und Weimar: Aufbau.

Vondung, Klaus. 1973. *Völkisch-nationale und nationalsozialistische Literaturtheorie*. Munich: List.

Wächter, Hans-Christof. 1973. *Theater im Exil: Sozialgeschichte des deutschen Exiltheaters 1933-1945*. Munich: Hanser.

Bahr, Ehrhard. 1974. "Die Bild- und Sinnbereiche von Feuer und Wasser in Lessings *Nathan der Weise*." *Lessing Yearbook* 6: 83-96.

Grimm, Gunter. 1974. "Lessing im Schullektüre-Kanon." *Germanisch Romanische Monatsschrift (Neue Folge)* 25 (1): 13-43.

Grimm, Reinhold. 1974. "Lessing — Ein Vorläufer Brechts? (Teil I)." *Lessing Yearbook* 6: 36-58.

Hohendahl, Peter Uwe, ed. 1974. *Sozialgeschichte und Wirkungsästhetik: Dokumente zur empirischen und marxistischen Rezeptionsforschung*. Frankfurt am Main: Athenäum.

König, Dominik von. 1974. "'Nathan der Weise' in der Schule: Ein Beitrag zur Wirkungsgeschichte Lessings." *Lessing Yearbook* 6: 108-138. Quoted from Bohnen 1984, 426-458.

Latta, Alan D. 1974. "Lessing and the Drug Scene: The 'bunte Blumen.' Metaphor in *Nathan der Weise*." *Lessing Yearbook* 6: 97-108.

Behler, Ernst, ed. 1975. *Kritische Friedrich-Schlegel-Ausgabe*. Vol. III. *Charakteristiken und Kritiken II (1802-1829)*. Ed. by Hans Eichner. Munich, Paderborn, and Vienna: Schöningh.

Grimm, Gunter. 1975. "Lessings Stil: Zur Rezeption eines kanonischen Urteils." In Grimm, ed. *Literatur und Leser: Theorien und Modelle zur Rezeption literarischer Werke*. Stuttgart: Reclam, 148-180.

Guthke, Karl S. 1975. "Grundlagen der Lessingforschung: Neuere Ergebnisse, Probleme, Aufgaben." In Schulz 1975, 10-46.

Heydemann, Klaus. 1975. "Gesinnung und Tat: Zu Lessings *Nathan der Weise.*" *Lessing Yearbook* 7: 69-104.

Kopitzsch, Franklin. 1975. "Lessing und Hamburg: Aspekte und Aufgaben der Forschung." *Wolfenbütteler Studien zur Aufklärung.* Vol. 2. Bremen, Wolfenbüttel: Jacobi Verlag, 47-120.

Schulte-Sasse, Jochen. 1975. *Literarische Struktur und historisch-sozialer Kontext: Zum Beispiel Lessings "Emilia Galotti."* Paderborn: Schöningh.

Schulz, Günter ed. 1975. *Wolfenbütteler Studien zur Aufklärung.* Vol. 2. Bremen and Wolfenbüttel: Jacobi Verlag.

Bauer, Gerhard. 1976. "Revision von Lessings 'Nathan': Anspruch, Strategie, Politik und Selbstverständnis der neuen Klassen." In Raitz and Schütz 1976, 69-108.

Guthke, Karl S. 1976. "Lessing und das Judentum: Rezeption. Dramatik und Kritik. Krypto-Spinozismus." [Lecture given in 1975 in Wolfenbüttel]. Quoted from Schulz 1977, 229-271.

König, Dominik von. 1976. *Natürlichkeit und Wirklichkeit: Studien zu Lessings "Nathan der Weise."* Bonn: Bouvier.

Lützeler, Paul Michael. 1976. "Die marxistische Lessing-Rezeption: II. Darstellung und Kritik am Beispiel der *Emilia Galotti*-Interpretation in der DDR." *Lessing Yearbook* 8: 42-60.

Raitz, Walter and Erhard Schütz, eds. 1976. *Der alte Kanon neu: Zur Revision des literarischen Kanons in Wissenschaft und Unterricht.* Opladen: Westdeutscher Verlag. (= Lesen 2).

Schnell, Josef. 1976. "Dramatische Struktur und soziales Handeln: Didaktische Überlegungen zur Lektüre von Lessings 'Nathan der Weise.'" *Der Deutschunterricht* 28 (2): 46-54. Quoted from Bohnen 1984, 459-471.

Träger, Claus. 1976. "Lessingsches Erbe." *Weimarer Beiträge* 22 (5): 80-96.

Göbel, Helmut, ed. 1977. *Lessings "Nathan": Der Autor, der Text, seine Umwelt, seine Folgen.* Berlin: Wagenbach.

Grimm, Gunter. 1977. *Rezeptionsgeschichte, Grundlegung einer Theorie: Mit Analysen und Bibliographie.* Munich: Fink.

Harris, Edward P. and Richard E. Schade, eds. 1977. *Lessing in heutiger Sicht: Beiträge zur Internationalen Lessing-Konferenz Cincinnati, Ohio 1976.* Bremen and Wolfenbüttel: Jacobi.

Höhle, Thomas. 1977. "Friedrich Schlegels Auseinandersetzung mit Lessing: Zum Problem des Verhältnisses zwischen Romantik und Aufklärung." *Weimarer Beiträge* 23 (2): 121-135.

Neumann, Peter Horst. 1977. *Der Preis der Mündigkeit: Über Lessings Dramen. Anhang: Über Fanny Hill.* Stuttgart: Klett-Cotta.

Pelters, Wilm. 1977. "Anti-Candide oder die Apotheose der Vorsehung." Quoted from Harris and Schade 1977, 251-258.

Schoeps, Julius H. 1977. "Aufklärung, Judentum und Emanzipation." In Günter Schulz 1977, 75-102.

Schulz, Günter, ed. 1977. *Wolfenbütteler Studien zur Aufklärung.* Vol. 4. *Judentum im Zeitalter der Aufklärung.* Bremen, Wolfenbüttel: Jacobi Verlag.

Schulz, Ursula. 1977. *Lessing auf der Bühne: Chronik der Theateraufführungen 1748-1789.* Bremen und Wolfenbüttel: Jacobi.

Steinmetz, Horst. 1977. "Gotthold Ephraim Lessing: Über die Aktualität eines umstrittenen Klassikers." Quoted from Harris and Schade 1977, 11-36.

Bollacher, Martin. 1978. *Lessing: Vernunft und Geschichte: Untersuchungen zum Problem religiöser Aufklärung in den Spätschriften.* Tübingen: Max Niemeyer.

Birus, Hendrik. 1978. *Poetische Namengebung: Zur Bedeutung der Namen in Lessings 'Nathan der Weise.'* Göttingen: Vandenhoeck & Ruprecht. (= Palaestra. Vol. 270). (Partial reprint in Bohnen 1984, 290-327).

Peter, Klaus. 1978. *Friedrich Schlegel.* Stuttgart: Metzler.

Schlütter, Hans-Jürgen. 1978. "'... als ob die Wahrheit Münze wäre': Zu *Nathan der Weise* III,6." *Lessing Yearbook* 10: 65-74.

Bohnen, Klaus. 1979. "'Nathan der Weise': Über das 'Gegenbild einer Gesellschaft' bei Lessing." *Deutsche Vierteljahrsschrift für Literaturwissenschaft und Geistesgeschichte* 53: 394-416.

Guthke, Karl S. [3]1979. *Gotthold Ephraim Lessing.* Stuttgart: Metzler. (First edition 1965).

Higonnet, Margaret R. 1979. "Friedrich Schlegel on Lessing: Criticism as the Mother of Poetics." *Lessing Yearbook* 11: 83-103.

Oelmüller, Willi. [2]1979. *Die unbefriedigte Aufklärung: Beiträge zu einer Theorie der Moderne von Lessing, Kant und Hegel.* Frankfurt am Main: Suhrkamp. First edition 1969.

Raschdau, Christine. 1979. *Die Aktualität der Vergangenheit: Zur gesellschaftlichen Relevanz der Lessing-Rezeption im 18. Jahrhundert und heute.* Königstein/Ts.: Forum Academicum in der Verlagsgruppe Athenäum, Hain, Scriptor, Hanstein. (= Hochschulschriften Literaturwissenschaft. Vol. 42).

Schütt, Peter. 1979. "Für die Pfeffersäcke hat der nicht gearbeitet: Lessing zum 250. Geburtstag." *Die Horen* 113: 18-19. Quoted from Dvoretzky 1981, 294-297.

Steinmetz, Horst, ed. 1979. *Gotthold Ephraim Lessings "Minna von Barnhelm": Dokumente zur Rezeptions- und Interpretationsgeschichte.* Königstein/Ts.: Athenäum. (= Athenäum Taschenbücher Literaturwissenschaft).

Wessels, Hans-Friedrich. 1979. *Lessings "Nathan der Weise": Seine Wirkungsgeschichte bis zum Ende der Goethezeit.* Königstein/Taunus: Athenäum.

Diederichsen, Diedrich and Bärbel Rudin, eds. 1980. *Lessing im Spiegel der Theaterkritik 1945 - 1979.* Berlin: Selbstverlag der Gesellschaft für Theatergeschichte.

Dierkes, Hans. 1980. *Literaturgeschichte als Kritik: Untersuchungen zu Theorie und Praxis von Friedrich Schlegels frühromantischer Literaturgeschichtsschreibung.* Tübingen: Niemeyer. (= Studien zur deutschen Literatur. Vol. 63).

Lecke, Bodo. 1980. *Literatur der deutschen Klassik: Rezeption und Wirkung.* Heidelberg: Quelle und Meyer. (= medium literatur 13).

Shoham, Chaim. 1980. "*Nathan der Weise* unter Seinesgleichen: Zur Rezeption Lessings in der hebräischen Literatur des 19. Jahrhunderts in Osteuropa." *Lessing Yearbook* 12: 1-30.

Stadelmaier, Gerhard. 1980. *Lessing auf der Bühne: Ein Klassiker im Theateralltag (1968-1974).* Tübingen: Max Niemeyer.

Suesse-Fiedler, Sigrid. 1980. *Lessings "Nathan der Weise" und seine Leser: Eine wirkungsästhetische Studie.* Stuttgart: Akademischer Verlag Hans-Dieter Heinz. (= Stuttgarter Arbeiten zur Germanistik. Vol. 80).

Werner, Hans-Georg. 1980. *Lessing-Konferenz Halle 1979.* 2 volumes. Halle: Martin-Luther-Universität.

Dvoretzky, Edward, ed. 1981. *Lessing heute: Beiträge zur Wirkungsgeschichte.* Stuttgart: Akademischer Verlag Hans-Dieter Heinz. (=Stuttgarter Arbeiten zur Germanistik. Vol. 87).

Eibl, Karl. 1981. "Gotthold Ephraim Lessing: Nathan der Weise." In Harro Müller-Michaels, ed. *Deutsche Dramen: Interpretationen zu Werken von der Aufklärung bis zur Gegenwart.* 2 volumes. Königstein/Ts.: Athenäum, Vol. 1, 3-30.

Göpfert, Herbert G., ed. 1981. *Das Bild Lessings in der Geschichte.* Heidelberg: Schneider. (= Wolfenbütteler Studien zur Aufklärung. Vol. 9).

Hasche, Christa. 1981. "'Über die Mehrheit der Welten': Anmerkungen und Überlegungen zu Lessings Rolle im Theater der DDR." *Weimarer Beiträge* 27 (9): 49-56.

Henning, Hans. 1981. *"Emilia Galotti" in der zeitgenössischen Rezeption.* Leipzig: Zentralantiquariat der Deutschen Demokratischen Republik. (= Werk und Wirkung. Dokumentationen zur deutschen Literatur. Vol. 2).

Raddatz, Fritz J. 1981. "Ein Bürger, ein Radikaler. Zum 200. Todestag: Nachdenken über Gotthold Ephraim Lessing." *Die Zeit* 8: 41-42. Quoted from Bohnen 1982, 123-133.

Schröder, Jürgen. 1981. "Der 'Kämpfer' Lessing." In Göpfert 1981, 93-114.

Strohschneider-Kohrs, Ingrid. 1981. "Die Vorstellung vom 'unpoetischen' Dichter Lessing." In Göpfert 1981, 13-35.

Türcke, Christoph. 1981. "Die geheime Kraft des Rings." *Merkur* 35 (2). Quoted from Bohnen 1982, 155-162.

Wangenheim, Inge von. 1981. "In seinem Leben, seinem Werk finden sich Denklust und Herz: Zum 200. Todestag Gotthold Ephraim Lessings." *Neues Deutschland* 14/15 (38). Quoted from Bohnen 1982, 169-172.

Werner, Hans-Georg. 1981. "Ideelle Formen der Lessing-Aneignung in der DDR." *Weimarer Beiträge* 27 (9): 5-48.

Bohnen, Klaus, ed. 1982. *Lessing: Nachruf auf einen Aufklärer. Sein Bild in der Presse der Jahre 1781, 1881 und 1981.* Munich: Fink.

Critchfield, Richard. 1982. "The Mixing of Old and New Wisdom: On Lessing's *Nathan der Weise* and Brecht's *Der kaukasische Kreidekreis.*" *Lessing Yearbook* 14: 161-175.

Holeczek, Heinz. 1982. "Die Judenemanzipation in Preußen." In Martin and Schulin [2]1982, 131-160.

Humboldt Universität. 1982. *Wirkungen Lessings in der deutschen Literatur: Beiträge zum Lessing-Kolloquium 1981 in Berlin. Wissenschaftliche Zeitschrift der*

Humboldt-Universität zu Berlin. (= Gesellschafts- und sprachwissenschaftliche Reihe. Vol 31 [5].)

Jens, Walter. May 10, 1982. "Nathan der Weise aus der Sicht von Auschwitz. Juden und Christen in Deutschland." In his *Kanzel und Katheder: Reden.* 1984. Munich: Kindler. 31-49.

Loiperdinger, Martin. 1982. "'Nathan der Weise': Faschistische Filmzensur. Antisemitismus und Gewalt anno 1923." *Lessing Yearbook* 14: 61-69.

Martin, Bernd and Ernst Schulin, eds. [2]1982. *Die Juden als Minderheit in der Geschichte.* Munich: dtv.

Zmarzlik, Hans-Günter. 1982. "Antisemitismus im Deutschen Kaiserreich 1871-1918. In Martin and Schulin [2]1982, 249-270.

Fuhrmann, Helmut. 1983. "Lessings *Nathan der Weise* und das Wahrheitsproblem. *Lessing Yearbook* 15: 63-94.

Albrecht, Wolfgang. 1984. "Lessing in Schillers Spätwerk." In Werner 1984, 218-233.

Bohnen, Klaus, ed. 1984. *Lessings "Nathan der Weise."* Darmstadt: Wissenschaftliche Buchgesellschaft. (= Wege der Forschung. Vol. 587).

Härtl, Heinz. 1984. "Wirkungen Lessings und Innovationen des deutschen Dramas zwischen 1789 und 1830." In Werner 1984, 183-217.

Hartung, Günter. 1984. "Die drei Ringe: Thesen zur Rezeptionsgeschichte des 'Nathan.'" In Werner 1984, 151-182.

Heinemann, Dieter. 1984. "Rezeption in der Arbeiterbewegung der Weimarer Republik." In Werner 1984, 361-400.

Höhle, Thomas. 1984. "Einige Wirkungen der Publizistik Lessings." In Werner 1984, 264-285.

Rieck, Werner. 1984. "Bürgerlich-demokratische Lessing-Aneignung (1910-1933)." In Werner 1984, 339-360.

Rüskamp, Wulf. 1984. *Dramaturgie ohne Publikum: Lessings Dramentheorie und die zeitgenössische Rezeption von "Minna von Barnhelm" und "Emilia Galotti." Ein Beitrag zur Geschichte des deutschen Theaters und seines Publikums.* Cologne and Vienna: Böhlau.

Werner, Hans-Georg, ed. 1984. *Bausteine zu einer Wirkungsgeschichte: Gotthold Ephraim Lessing.* Berlin und Weimar: Aufbau.

Berghahn, Klaus L. 1985. "Von der klassizistischen zur klassischen Literaturkritik." In Hohendahl 1985a, 10-75.

Berman, Russel A. 1985. "Literaturkritik zwischen Reichsgründung und 1933." In Hohendahl 1985a, 205-274.

Hohendahl, Peter Uwe. 1985a. *Geschichte der deutschen Literaturkritik (1730-1980)*. Stuttgart: Metzler.

——. 1985b. *Literarische Kultur im Zeitalter des Liberalismus: 1830 - 1870*. Munich: Beck.

Zimmermann, Bernhard. 1985. "Entwicklung der deutschen Literaturkritik von 1933 bis zur Gegenwart." In Hohendahl 1985a, 275-338.

Boeser, Knut and Renata Vatkova. 1986. *Erwin Piscator: Eine Arbeitsbiographie*. Vol. 2. *Moskau — Paris — New York — Berlin. 1931-1966*. Berlin: Hentrich.

Detering, Heinrich. 1986. "Christian Wilhelm Dohm und die Idee der Toleranz." In Freimark, Kopitzsch and Slessarev 1986, 174-185.

Freimark, Peter, Franklin Kopitzsch, and Helga Slassarev, eds. 1986. *Lessing und die Toleranz: Beiträge der vierten internationalen Konferenz der Lessing Society in Hamburg vom 27. bis 29. Juni 1985. Sonderdruck zum Lessing Yearbook*. Detroit and Munich: Wayne State Univ. Press.

Kahn, Ludwig W. 1986. "The Changing Image of the Jew: Nathan the Wise and Shylock." In Mark H. Gelber, ed. *Identity and Ethos: A Festschrift for Sol Liptzin on the Occasion of His 85th Birthday*. New York and Bern: Lang. 235-252.

Kreft, Jürgen. 1986. "Lessing und die Toleranz — Toleranzerziehung und Literatur- unterricht." In Freimark, Kopitzsch and Slassarev 1986, 209-221.

Moses, Stéphane and Albrecht Schöne, eds. 1986. *Juden in der deutschen Literatur: Ein deutsch-israelisches Symposion*. Frankfurt am Main: Suhrkamp.

Specht, Rolf. 1986. *Die Rhetorik in Lessings "Anti-Goeze": Ein Beitrag zur Phänomenolgie der Polemik*. Bern, Frankfurt am Main and New York: Lang. (=Europäische Hochschulschriften. Deutsche Sprache und Literatur. Vol. 937).

Stenzel, Jürgen. 1986. "Idealisierung und Vorurteil: Zur Figur des 'edlen Juden' in der deutschen Literatur des 18. Jahrhunderts." In Moses and Schöne 1986, 114-126.

Zimmermann, Moshe. 1986. "'Lessing contra Sem': Literatur im Dienste des Antisemitismus." In Moses and Schöne 1986, 179-193.

Barner, Wilfried, Gunter Grimm, Helmut Kiesel, and Martin Kramer, eds. [5]1987. *Lessing. Epoche — Werk — Wirkung*. Munich: Beck. (First edition 1975).

Bauer, Gerhard. 1987. *Gotthold Ephraim Lessing: "Emilia Galotti."* Munich: Fink.

Habermas, Jürgen. [17]1987. *Strukturwandel der Öffentlichkeit: Untersuchungen zu einer Kategorie der bürgerlichen Gesellschaft*. Darmstadt: Luchterhand (First edition 1962).

Heller, Agnes. 1987. "Aufklärung gegen Fundamentalismus: Der Fall Lessing." *Lessing Yearbook* 19: 29-44.

Lauf-Immesberger, Karin. 1987. *Literatur, Schule und Nationalsozialismus*. St. Ingbert: Röhrig.

Leventhal, Robert S. 1987. "The Parable as Performance: Interpretation, Cultural Transmission and Political Strategy in Lessing's *Nathan der Weise*." *German Quarterly* 61 (4): 502-527.

Piedmont, Ferdinand. 1987. "Unterdrückt und rehabilitiert: Zur Theatergeschichte von Lessings *Nathan der Weise* von den zwanziger Jahren bis zur Gegenwart." *Lessing Yearbook* 19: 85-94.

Kuhles, Doris. 1988. *Lessing-Bibliographie 1971-1985*. Berlin and Weimar: Aufbau.

Wurst, Karin A. 1988. *Familiale Liebe ist die 'wahre Gewalt': Die Repräsentation der Familie in G.E. Lessings dramatischem Werk*. Amsterdam: Rodopi. (= Amsterdamer Publikationen zur Sprache und Literatur. Vol. 75).

Kowalik, Jill Anne. 1989. "*Nathan der Weise* as Lessing's Work of Mourning." *Lessing Yearbook* 21: 1-17.

Timm, Eitel. 1989. *Ketzer und Dichter: Lessing, Goethe, Thomas Mann und die Postmoderne in der Tradition des Häresiegedankens*. Heidelberg: Winter.

Wulf, Joseph. 1989. *Literatur und Dichtung im Dritten Reich: Eine Dokumentation*. Frankfurt am Main and Berlin: Ullstein.

Albrecht, Wolfgang. 1990. "Lessing Forschung 1984 bis 1988: Ein Literaturbericht auf der Grundlage ausgewählter Publikationen." *Weimarer Beiträge* 36 (7): 1164-1180.

Arendt, Hannah. [8]1990. *Rahel Varnhagen. Lebensgeschichte einer deutschen Jüdin aus der Romantik*. Munich and Zurich: Piper.

Arendt, Dieter. [4]1990. *Gotthold Ephraim Lessing: Nathan der Weise*. Frankfurt am Main: Diesterweg. (First edition 1984). (= Grundlagen und Gedanken zum Verständnis des Dramas).

Hildebrandt, Dieter. 1990. *Lessing: Eine Biographie*. Hamburg: Rowohlt (First edition 1979).

Michelsen, Peter. 1990. *Der unruhige Bürger: Studien zu Lessing und zur Literatur des achtzehnten Jahrhunderts*. Würzburg: Königshausen und Neumann.

Rose, Paul Lawrence. 1990. *Revolutionary Antisemitism in Germany: From Kant to Wagner*. Princeton: Princeton University Press.

Eckardt, Jo-Jacqueline. 1991. "Das Lessingbild im Dritten Reich." *Lessing Yearbook* 23: 69-78.

Lea, Charlene A. 1991. "Tolerance Unlimited: 'The Noble Jew' on the German and Austrian Stage (1750-1805)." *German Quarterly* 64 (2): 166-177.

Simon, Rolf. 1991. "Nathans Argumentationsverfahren: Konsequenzen der Fiktionalisierung von Theorien in Lessings Drama *Nathan der Weise*." *Deutsche Vierteljahrsschrift für Literaturwissenschaft und Geistesgeschichte* 65 (4): 609-35.

Der Spiegel. November 18, 1991. "Gescheiterter Narr. George Taboris jüngste Arbeit: 'Nathans Tod', eine Szenencollage, die dem Humanismus Lessings aktuelle Bilder des Schreckens entgegensetzt." 47 (45): 322-323.

Wille, Franz. 1991. "Klassikerkommentar x Regieautor = Zeittheater?: Nathans Not. George Taboris Lessing-Variation, uraufgeführt in Wolfenbüttel." *Theater heute* 12: 2-5.

Index